MirrorWORD

The incarnation is the most accurate and articulate translation.

Any sincere student of classical music would sensitively seek to capture and interpret the piece, so as not to distract from the original sound of the composition.

To form a conclusion in the study of our origin would involve a peering over the Creator's shoulder as it were, in order to gaze through his eyes and marvel at his anticipation. His invisible image and likeness is about to be unveiled in human form!

The incarnation celebrates the fact that the destiny of the Word was not the page but tangible human life! The word of truth preserves God's original idea in the resonance of our hearts.

2 Corinthians 3:2 Instead of an impressive certificate framed on my wall I have you framed in my heart! You are our Epistle written within us, an open letter speaking a global language; one that everyone can [1]read and recognize as their mother tongue! (The word [1]**anaginosko**, from **ana**, upward and **ginosko**, to know upward; thus to draw knowledge from a higher reference; from above; to recognize; to read with recognition.)

2 Corinthians 3:3 The fact that you are a Christ-Epistle shines as bright as day! This is what our ministry is all about. The Spirit of God is the living ink. Every trace of the Spirit's influence on the heart is what gives permanence to this conversation. We are not talking law-language here; this is more dynamic and permanent than letters chiseled in stone. This conversation is embroidered in your inner consciousness. (It is the life of your design that grace echoes within you!)

Behold how beautiful
how valuable
how loved
you are!

This is the first of 3 volumes containing 8 chapters each of the magnificent, Dr. Luke's Gospel!

Editing preparation for printing: Sean Osmond

Mirror Word Logo by: Wilna Furstenburg

Cover Design by: Sean Osmond

Published by Mirror Word Publishing

Should you wish to order printed copies in bulk, [2 or more] pls contact us at info@mirrorword.net

Contact us if you wish to help sponsor Mirror Bibles in Spanish, Shona or Xhosa.

Highly recommended books by the same author: Divine Embrace, God Believes in You, The Logic of His Love.

Children's books: The Eagle Story, by Lydia and Francois du Toit, illustrated by Carla Krige

Stella's Secret by Lydia du Toit and illustrated by Wendy Francisco. Also in German.

Lydia has also released 2 more beautiful children's stories, The Little Bear and The Mirror and her latest book, Kaa!

The Mirror Bible, Divine Embrace God Believes in You and The Logic of His Love are also available on Kindle. The new updated Mirror Bible App is avaiable on our website

www.mirrorword.net

Subscribe to Francois facebook updates http://www.facebook.com/francois.toit

The Mirror Translation fb group http://www.facebook.com/groups/179109018883718/

ISBN 978-0-9922236-8-7

THE MIRROR STUDY BIBLE

The Mirror Study Bible is a paraphrased translation from the Greek text. While strictly following the literal meaning of the original, sentences have been constructed so that the larger meaning is continually emphasized by means of an expanded text.

Some clarifying notes are included in italics. This is a paraphrased study rather than a literal translation. While the detailed shades of meaning of every Greek word and its components have been closely studied, this is done taking into account the consistent context of the entire chapter within the wider epistle, and bearing in mind that Jesus is what the Scriptures are all about and humankind is what Jesus is all about.

To assist the reader in their study, I have numerically superscripted the Greek word and corresponded it with the closest English word in the italicized commentary that follows. This is to create a direct comparison of words between the two languages.

I translated several Pauline epistles in the eighties but these were never published.

In 2007 I started with the Mirror Translation. This is an ongoing process and will eventually include the entire New Testament as well as select portions of the Old Testament.

Completed books and chapters as of May 2020 are:

John's Gospel, Romans, 1 Corinthians, 2 Corinthians,

Galatians, Ephesians, Philippians, Colossians,

1 Thessalonians, 2 Timothy, Titus, Hebrews, James, 1 Peter 1,2, 2 Peter 1

1 John 1-5, Luke 1-16,

Revelation

In the Mirror,
Bible language becomes heart to heart
whispers of grace!

Jesus Christ, the Incarnation, mankind's co-inclusion,
co-crucifixion, co-resurrection and co-seatedness in him, is the
only valid context and theme of Scripture.

This is the good of the Good News!

Jesus exhibits the Father and the Holy Spirit in one man,

in action!

Jesus is God's language and message to mankind.

To add anything to his completed work in revealing and
redeeming the image of God in human form,

or take anything away from what God spoke to us in him,

is to depart from the essence of the Gospel.

There is no perfect translation,

there is only a perfect Word: the Logic of God.

The Bible is all about Jesus.

What makes the book irresistibly relevant, is the fact that

Jesus is all about you!

God has found a face in you that portrays him

more beautifully than the best theology!

Your features, your touch, the cadence of your voice,

the compassion in your gaze, the lines of your smile,

the warmth of your person and presence unveil him!

INDEX

The Mirror Bible is a work in progress

The Ninth edition - is a 944 page book which is also available on Kindle or as an App in Android as well as in Apple.

The following individual books are also separately available,

Revelation, Romans, Hebrews, Philippians and Vol 1 and Vol 2 of three Volumes of Luke (8 Chapters each)

www.mirrorword.net

Reflecting on any translation of Scripture gives one the opportunity to hear our Maker's voice and thoughts, filtered through the interpretation and language of the translator(s).

In this fresh Paraphrase, Francois du Toit has opened the curtain for readers of any age, culture or language to enjoy amazing insights into the heartbeat of *Agape* - where everyone feels equally loved, included and valued in the eyes of the Father - and fully redeemed in the union we come from! The Mirror underlines the fact that we did not merely begin in our mother's womb; we are the invention and idea of God!

To have this work now also available in Xhosa will mark a new era for young and old to rediscover the Bible afresh.

Archbishop **DESMOND TUTU** - *Legacy Foundation*

The Mirror Bible is a transforming paraphrased translation that is simplistic, accurate, detailed and comprehensive, captivating and at the same time exuding intriguing spiritual revelation; it is divinely insightful and contemporary.

It's a must read, a befitting guide and manual for all age groups for; Bible study, meditation, devotion, worship, teaching, instruction and scholarship.

Jesus Christ is the epicenter of the entire text.

Believers will not miss the centrality of the translation as there is a finite and delicate thread directing to the revealing and redeeming Christ.

Unbelievers will derive unrivaled comfort from the text as they get captivated by the reality and close proximity of Christ.

This is definitely a life giving and transforming translation. I am humbly convinced that Francois is chosen by God to serve this generation and the next with undiluted truth in the midst of incomprehensible compromises of worldly, heretical and traditional, doctrinal interpretations and practices (religion) that have diverted us from the truth.

The Mirror Bible is a welcome revelatory and revolutionary development that is divinely sanctioned, inspired and directed. This translation is by no doubt a compelling grounding expository of our century.
To God be the Glory.

Rev. **ANOUYA ANDREW MUCHECHETERE**, *MBA, MA,*
Former Secretary General of the Evangelical Fellowship of Zimbabwe (EFZ).

The mystery concerning God's Own action in Christ, balanced with the nature and necessity of our human response has defined my personal journey for many years.

When I was introduced to Francois du Toit and the Mirror Bible, much of that mystery were resolved. Often, I found myself 'gasping for breath' as some new aspect of the mystery of Christ and His Kingdom emerged with startling clarity.

Francois' love for the text, his sheer exegetical courage and his astonishing ability to express essential biblical pre-suppositions in the intimate Love language of God, has opened for Judith and me a renewed and trans-formative biblical understanding.

BOB and **JUDITH MUMFORD** - www.lifechangers.org

The Mirror Translation is astonishingly beautiful. The union theme is outstanding.

The early followers of Jesus knew that he was the center of all creation, the plan from the beginning, the alpha and the omega, the author and finisher of faith. They wrestled deeply with these questions and the stag-gering implications of Jesus's very identity. They handed down clear and powerful and very relevant insights and answers. Francois has met the Jesus of the Apostles, and through his wrestling with their light, is providing for us all a paraphrase of their work that is as thrilling as it is beautiful and true.

My imagination ignites reading your translation. What a beautiful, breathtaking translation. This is brilliant, and destined to relieve and liberate many. You sing the Father's heart, my brother. May the Holy Spirit continue to use the Mirror to reveal Jesus and his Father and us all around this world! I love it.

This first volume of Luke is so beautiful! Poetic and profound. You must keep going dear brother!

DR. C. BAXTER KRUGER *Author of "The Great Dance" and "The Shack Revisited"*

In a world where Bible translations and paraphrases are ubiquitous, *The Mirror Study Bible* is uniquely beautiful and helpful! Submitted to the original texts and the abiding guidance of the Holy Spirit, Francois du Toit carefully and meticulously opens and explores the treasures of Scripture. Not only does it satisfy the demands of the intellect, but it overwhelms the heart.

WM PAUL YOUNG - *Author of The Shack*

I have been asked at times why God didn't make the Bible easier to understand. If He is able to inspire the writings of Scripture, couldn't He provide a key for unlocking its treasures for us? *The Mirror Translation* you hold in your hand opens the treasure-chest of understanding with that Key. The key to properly understanding the Bible is Jesus Christ. He is the source and subject of its pages. For years I have been asked why there isn't a Bible translation that presents the Scriptures from a pure grace orientation. It is a great encouragement to know that the Mirror Bible is just that. Drawing not only from the literal meaning, but also the historical nuances of the Greek language, Francois Du Toit presents this translation in a way that will enrich your love for our Triune God and ground you in the grace expressed to us all through Jesus Christ. This is a translation you will read again and again. It is one you will share with your friends.

DR. STEVE McVEY - *Founder of Grace Walk Ministries, Florida*

The Bible is God's amazing conversation with us. Here we engage with God's words that crescendo in the revelation of his Son, Jesus Christ. The greatest joy is to realize that you as an individual are included in this conversation.

This translation is in all probability one of the greatest contributions in the last few years to the broader church. It is imperative that every Christ follower discovers their true identity mirrored in Jesus. The most liberating revelation is the fact that we have not only died together with Him, but that we were also raised with Him in resurrection life. Then to grasp that we are seated with Him in heavenly places, where we may now live our daily lives from a position of significance and influence within this world. The premise of the Good News of the Gospel is that we are not required to strive to attain something through personal achievement, but rather to discover who we already are and what we already have in Christ, as revealed in the glorious Scriptures.

May The Mirror Translation impact your life as much as it has mine, and may it facilitate your spiritual journey to truly relocate your mind, living from the new vantage point of this glorious life in Christ.

ALAN Platt - *Visionary leader of* **Doxa Deo** *International*

My philosophy in doing the Mirror Bible is reflected in the following example:

I do not read music, but have often witnessed our son, Stefan, approach a new piece on the piano.

His eyes see so much more than mere marks scribbled on a page;

he hears the music.

His trained mind engages even the subtleties and the nuances of the original composition, and is able to repeat the authentic sound,

knowing that the destiny of the music would never be reduced to the page;

but is always in the next moment,

where the same intended beauty is heard, and repeated again!

The best translation would always be the incarnation!

I so value the enormity of the revelation of the incarnation.

Yet, before flesh, the Word was προς

face to face with God!

And fragile text

scribbled through the ages in memoirs of stone, parchment and papyrus pages

carrying eternity in thought

and continues to translate faith

to faith!

Now we have the same spirit of faith as he encountered when he wrote...

"I believe

and so I speak!"

Conversation ignites!

Did not our hearts burn within our being when He spoke familiar text of ancient times, in the voices of Moses and the prophets and David and Abraham,

who saw his day

and announced its dawn in our hearts!

The mystery that was hidden for ages and generations

is now revealed!

In dealing daily with ancient text,

rediscovering thoughts buried in time, I am often overwhelmed and awed at the magnificence of eternity captured in little time capsules,

opening vistas of beauty beyond our imagination -

face to face with the same face to faceness of the Logos

and God

and us - conceived in their dream!

And irresistibly intrigued by the invitation to come and drink -

to taste and see -

from the source -

and to hear a saint reminiscing and reminding himself of the utterance of another earth dweller-brother, David, who wrote a song 3000 years ago,

"Return to your rest oh my soul!

For the Lord has dealt bountifully with you!

I believe and so I speak!"

And with fresh wounds bleeding from the many angry blows he was dealt with, Paul echoes,

"We have the same spirit of faith as he had who wrote, 'I believe and so I speak!' We too believe and so we speak!"

Let's celebrate the "sameness" of Jesus

yesterday - yes, as far as history and beyond time can go -

and today! This very finite, fragile moment -

plus the infinite future!

Inexhaustible, beyond boundaries and the confines of space and time!

Introcution to Luke

I have absolutely fallen in love with Dr. Luke! This dear, humble companion of Paul is a giant of a man, both in his account of Jesus, as well as that of the early church in the book of Acts! Luke is the longest book in the New Testament. Nearly half of the content of his account of Jesus, is unique to him. He is also the one Gospel writer who highlights the many times Jesus honored women.

Here is an extract from Marvin Vincent's observation in his *"Introduction to his Word Studies in Luke." [Kindle] Vincent was a 19-century Presbyterian minister and professor of New Testament at Union Theological Seminary in New York City.*

Luke represents the views of Paul, as Mark does of Peter. "There is a striking resemblance between the style of Luke and of Paul, which corresponds to their spiritual sympathy and long intimacy." Some two hundred expressions or phrases may be found which are common to Luke and Paul, and more or less foreign to other New Testament writers. Both are fond of words characterizing the freedom and universality of the gospel of salvation. For example, χάρις, *charis*, grace, favor, occurs eight times in the Gospel, sixteen in the Acts, and ninety-five in Paul. Then, *eleos*, ελεος, mercy, six times in the Gospel and ten in Paul. Also, πίστις, *pistis*, faith, twenty-seven times in the Gospel and Acts, and everywhere in Paul. Compare also δικαιοσύνη, *dikaiosune*, righteousness; δίκαιος, *dikaios*, righteous; πνεῦμα ἅγιον, *pneuma hagion*, Holy Spirit; γνῶσις, *gnosis*, knowledge.

Luke's is the universal gospel. His Gospel is for the Gentiles. The genealogy of Jesus, the Messiah, is traced back to the common father of the race, Adam, instead of to Abraham, the father of the Jewish nation, as by Matthew.

Luke records the enrolment of Jesus as a citizen of the Roman empire. Simeon greets him as a light for revelation to the Gentiles. The Baptist cites concerning him Isaiah's prophecy that all flesh shall see the salvation of God.

Luke alone records the mission of the seventy two, who represent the seventy two Gentile nations, *[According to Jewish tradition, there were seventy-two different language groups in the world]*, as the twelve represent the twelve tribes of Israel. He alone mentions the mission of Elijah to the heathen widow, and Naaman's cleansing by Elisha. He contrasts the gratitude of the one Samaritan leper with the thanklessness of the nine Jewish lepers. He alone records the refusal to call down fire on the inhospitable Samaritans, and the parable of the Good Samaritan is peculiar to him. He notes the commendation of the humble Publican in contrast with the self-righteous Pharisee, and relates how Jesus abode with Zacchaeus.

He omits all reference to the law in the Sermon on the Mount. Luke's is the gospel of the poor and outcast. As a phase of its universality, the humblest and most sinful are shown as not excluded from Jesus. The highest heavenly honor is conferred on the humble Mary of Nazareth. Luke and Paul also agree in their report of the Lord's Supper, both giving "This cup is the new covenant in my blood," for "This is my blood of the new covenant," and both adding, "in remembrance of me."

A few of the numerous instances of parallelism of thought and expression may also be cited: Asia Minor; and, with the exception of Hippocrates, all the extant Greek medical writers were Asiatic Greeks. Hippocrates, indeed, can hardly be called an exception, as he was born and lived in the island of Cos, off the coast of Caria. Galen was of Pergamus in Mysia; Dioscorides, of Anazarba in Cilicia; and Aretaeus, of Cappadocia. The medical peculiarities of Luke's style appear, first, in words and phrases used in descriptions of diseases or of miracles of healing. His terms are of the technical character peculiar to a medical man. Thus, in the account of the healing of Simon's wife's mother (Luk 4:38, Luk 4:39), we read that she was taken (συνεχομένη) with a great fever (πυρετῷ μεγάλῳ). The word taken is used nine times by Luke, and only three times in the rest of the New Testament. It occurs frequently in this sense in the medical writers, as does also the simple verb ἔχω, to have or hold. Moreover, according to Galen, the ancient physicians were accustomed to distinguish between great and little fevers. In the parable of the rich man and Lazarus (Luk 16: 19-26), we find εἱλκωμένος, full of sores, the regular medical term for to be ulcerated: ὀδυνῶμαι, to be in pain, occurs four times in Luke's writings, and nowhere else in the New Testament, but frequently in Galen, Aretaeus, and Hippocrates. Ἐξέψυξε, "gave up the spirit" [ghost], (Act 5: 5, Act 5: 10), is a rare phrase, used by Luke only, and occurring only three times in the New Testament. It seems to be almost confined to medical writers, and to be used rarely even by them. In the proverb of "the camel and the needle's eye," Matthew and Mark use for needle the ordinary word ῥαφίς, while Luke alone uses βελόνη, the surgical needle.

12

1:1 There has been several attempts to give an [1]accurate account of the [2]extent of that which has been fully accomplished [3]within us. *(The word, διηγησιν, diegesin, an accurate account; from διά, dia through, and ἡγέομαι, hegeomai, to lead or carry a narration through to the end; to lead with distinction; with the idea of thoroughness. A strengthened form of the word agoo, to lead; thus, to be officially appointed in a position of authority. Dr. Luke was familiar with this terminology. The word was particularly applied to a medical treatise. Galen applies it at least seventy-three times to the writings of Hippocrates. [Vincent]*

Having travelled extensively with Paul, Luke gets to the core of the good news in his opening statement! Not only are we audience to these events but indeed, in the unveiling of the mystery, we are the immediate beneficiaries of its consequence. In the incarnation revelation, the entire human race has been greatly advantaged! The ultimate significance of the Christ-event is not merely its historic relevance, but therein, that it will forever be celebrated in the unfolding of the mystery of the ages - which is [1]Christ, unveiled in human life, in the nations as well as in every individual. This unveiling is what transforms society into bridal bliss! The New Jerusalem is not a city but the redeemed society of mankind! The Bride of Christ! See my notes on the City Bride in Rev 3.

The words, [3]en hemin, 'in us' say so much more than merely 'amongst us'! πεπληροφορημένων ἐν ἡμῖν πραγμάτων peplerophoremenoon having been fully accomplished en hemin in us pragmatoon. The Genitive Case [-oon endings in verb and noun], confirms that this matter belongs to us!

The word, [2]plērophoreō, to fully accomplish, is the Perfect Passive Participle in the Genitive case, peplerophoremenoon. The Passive Participle describes a state that exists at the time coincident with that of the leading verb [epecheiresan Aorist Active Indicative to give accurate account] as a result of an action completed prior to the time of the main verb; the basic thought of the perfect tense is that the progress of an action has been completed and the results of the action are continuing on, in full effect. In other words, the progress of the action has reached its culmination and the finished results are now present.)

1:2 Exactly as it has been handed down to us by those who were eyewitnesses [1]since the beginning and therefore, [2]under-rowers and pioneers in carrying the precious cargo of the Word. *(These eyewitnesses include the [1]prophetic carriers of the promise! The word,*

[2]*huperetes*, *means an under-rower, who was one who was in the trireme, quadrireme, or quinquereme galleys and rowed in one of the undermost benches; they were often the least visible part of the whole operation, but most significant in their contribution! See 1 Cor 4:1)*

1:3 I too determined to acquaint myself thoroughly with the utmost attention to detail, scrutinising the unfolding of everything with fresh insight from a [1]heavenly perspective. And thus, I produced this written record with you in mind, most honorable [2]friend of God! *(The Adverb, [1]anōthen, means, from above. [2]Theopholis could also be an individual's name - it means, friend of God. Luke directs his book of Acts to the same "Friend of God".)*

1:4 My prayer is that this word will be a [1]heavenly download into your spirit so that you may know [2]beyond a shadow of a doubt the absolute certainty of these things that you were taught. *(The verb, [1]katēchēthēs, is in the first Aorist Passive Indicative form. This word is not in the LXX [Greek O.T.] and rare in ancient Greek. It occurs in the papyri. From **kata**, downwards and **echos**, a sound; thus **katēcheō** speaks of the roar of the waves of the sea; to sound down upon into the ears; to resound; to charm with resounding sound; to fascinate; to teach orally; to instruct; to inform by word of mouth. Certainty; secure; without a doubt; [2]**asphaleia** ἀσφάλεια from the negative particle, **a** and **sphallo**, to make no slip; without fail. In God's desire to persuade us, every possible margin for error, doubt or dispute is taken out of the equation! Heb 6:17)*

1:5 The following event occurred during the reign of Herod over Judea. There was a priest, Zechariah, of the [1]Abijah division whose turn it was to do the daily temple service. He was married to Elizabeth, a descendent of Aaron. *(Abijah* אביה *- Jaweh is my Abba!)*

1:6 They were both living exemplary and righteous lives [1]before God. *(The word, [1]enantion, from en, in and anti, in the presence of, over against - mirrored in.)*

1:7 Since Elizabeth was barren they could not have children and were now already advanced in years.

1:8 It so happened that while his division of priests were on temple duty before God,

1:9 he was allotted with the once in a lifetime opportunity of a priest to prepare and present the perfume on the altar of incense before the veil of the Most Holy inner sanctuary. *(Zechariah belonged to the priestly division of Abijah and was one of about 18,000 priests in Israel at the time; the descendants of Aaron of the tribe of Levi. In 1 Chronicles 24 there is a listing of the divisions of the priests. There are twenty-four divisions amongst the priests listed. [1 Chron 7-17] The particular division to which they belonged, would be on duty in the temple for just two weeks every year.*

Lots were drawn to decide who the handful of men would be to travel to Jerusalem. Usually just once in a man's entire lifetime would he be on duty in the temple. The Mishnah actually mentions five priests out of the 350 of each division, serving for the two weeks inside the temple, three of them looking after the lamp and the showbread while the other two served at the altar of incense. This group of men left their homes to live in Jerusalem for two weeks in the priests' accommodation to work in the temple. Then at the end of each service, morning and evening, Zechariah and his four friends would come out of the temple and stand on the top of the steps facing the multitudes of praying people who had gathered in silence around the altar in the outer court. There they would say the benediction, "The LORD bless you and keep you; the LORD make his face shine upon you and be gracious to you; the LORD turn his face towards you and give you peace" Numbers 6:24-26. Geoff Thomas)

1:10 During the hour of incense, the people of Israel would be in solemn prayer outside. *(See my commentary notes in Rev 8:1-5. "There is a strong allusion to different parts of the temple worship. While the priest went in to burn incense in the holy place, all the people continued in silent prayer without till the priest returned. The Angel [celestial shepherd-messenger] mentioned here appears to execute the office of priest." Adam Clarke.)*

1:11 Suddenly, to the right of the altar of incense in front of the veil between the Holy and Most Holy place, a messenger of the Lord appeared to him.

1:12 Zechariah was shocked and very afraid! *(There has been no record of any such manifestation or divine encounter in Israel for 400 years! God's silence was obviously interpreted as a sign of pending judgment - therefore the great shock when the messenger showed up with good news!)*

1:13 The messenger, standing before him said, [1]Jah is mindful, Zechariah, you have no reason to fear! This is the moment for your dream to [2]realize! Elizabeth shall bear you a son and you shall name him John. *(The Hebrew meaning of [1]Zecahriah is, Jah is mindful! His wife, Elizabeth's name, is also the name of Aaron's wife; אלישבע means, Elohim is my oath - the guarantee of my persuasion. See notes on the Oath at the end of Rev 10.*

As the officiating priest, it was Zechariah's job to place incense on the altar, heated with coals from the brazen altar of sacrifice and then prostrate himself in prayer. The incense represented the prayers of the people. Outside, the people were reciting this prayer during the incense offering: "May the merciful God enter the Holy Place and accept with favor the offering of his people."

If we render the Aorist literally, εισηκουσθη [2]eisekousthe, "was heard", we avoid the question as to what prayer is referred to. The reference is to the prayer for offspring, which, owing to his extreme years, Zechariah had probably ceased to offer, and which he certainly would not prefer in that public and solemn service. Hence the Aorist is appropriate, referring back to the past acts of prayer. "That prayer, which you no longer pray, was heard." Vincent's Word Studies.

*Zechariah is about to be startled to his core by the mercy and favor of God! Here he stands in this most solemn, once in a lifetime moment, representing the entire sacrificial system and tradition, imploring the God of Israel with sacrifice and sweet smelling incense! And he, who felt so disqualified to have a child - guilt ridden because of a system founded in sin consciousness - now has to process this heavenly encounter of God's favor! The name of this miracle child will be a constant reminder and endorsement of the favor of Elohim! The Greek name Ιωαννης **Ioannes**, derives from the Hebrew name **Yochanan** - יהוחנן Jaweh is gracious. John embodies the grace of God in his person and mission.*

Yochanan, Jaweh's mercy, would introduce and unveil the Lamb of God, who would take away the sin of the world! This is unheard of - the entire prophetic priesthood and their sacrificial system is about to be rendered redundant! This is not about a God demanding a sacrifice, but God being the sacrifice and concluding the judgment of the cosmos in his death and resurrection!)

1:14 And there will be a festivity of delight with much leaping and dancing as multitudes rejoice at his birth! *(The word, **agalliasisis** is only used in the LXX and the New Testament*

- *it means extreme exultation. From* **agan** *[much] and* **hallomai** *to jump with joy!)*

1:15 His stature of greatness will be in a life of face to face encounter in the presence of the Lord. His jubilant intoxication will not be by wine or strong drink, but by the indwelling Holy Spirit, even in his mother's womb!

1:16 And he will turn the [1]mass of the sons of Israel to the Lord their God. *(The word,* **polus,** *multitudes or all together, from* **pas,** *all; the whole. See the use of both* **pas** *and* **polus** *in Acts 26:29.)*

1:17 In the same prophetic spirit and power of Elijah, he will go before the face of the one he's about to introduce! And turn the hearts of the fathers to the children! And will convert their unbelief into a seeing for themselves, by bringing them to an unveiled understanding of righteousness. Thus, [1]preparing people's minds for a seamless transition into everything that the prophets pointed to which is now accomplished in the Lord, in a face to face encounter. The [2]meticulously detailed engineering of mankind's salvation is about to be fully realized! *(See also Luke 1:76. "A little child shall guide them" Isa 11:1-10 LXX. The fathers are blind, and have lost their voice, as pictured here in Zechariah's own unbelief - he might have given up on his dream to have a son, but God hasn't! Zechariah 1:4 Be not like your fathers, to whom the former prophets cried out! The "fathers" represent the gen-erations of Jews who continued in the blindfold mode of their own unenlightened unbelief. This is the end of an era; a new generation is introduced. "In many and various ways God spoke of old to our fathers through the prophets, but now, in the conclusion of the ages, God has spoken to us in sonship-language!" Heb 1:1.*

2 Cor 4:4 The survival and self-improvement programs of the religious systems of this world veil the minds of the unbelievers; exploiting their ignorance about their true origin and their redeemed innocence. The veil of unbelief obstructs a person's view and keeps them from seeing what the light of the gospel so clearly reveals: the glory of God is the image and likeness of our Maker redeemed in human form; this is what the gospel of Christ is all about.

In the dynamic spirit of Elijah - **en pneumati kai dunamei Eleiā.** *See Isaiah 40:1-11; Mal 3:1-5; also Mal 4:5,6. John will deny that he is actually Elijah in person, as they expected [Joh 1:21], but Jesus will call him Elijah in spirit [Mar 9:12; Mat 17:12]. Robertson's word pictures.*

The word [1]hetoimazō suggests a preparing of a highway. From the oriental custom of sending people ahead to level the roads and make them passable before a king's journey. What seemed a cul-de-sac for the flesh is a royal highway for faith. [Isaiah 40:3-5] See Luke 1:79. Then follows the word κατεσκευασμενον *[2]kateskeuasmenon, as in the building of a super structure; Luke often uses the Perfect Passive Participle which is a hebraistic equivalent for the superlative.)*

1:18 And Zechariah said to the messenger, "How can this possibly be! My wife and I are far too old!"

1:19 And the messenger responded, "I am [1]Gabriel; as my name suggests, I am representing the powerful [2]presence of God. I have been specifically assigned to engage you [[3]pros] and announce to you this wonderful news!" *(The [2]Preposition* **para,** *indicates close proximity; a thing proceeding from a sphere of influence, with a suggestion of union of place of residence; to have sprung from its author and giver; originating from; denoting the point from which an action originates; intimate connection. The word [2]enopion,* ενωπιον *is literally in the face of; in the immediate presence of. The preposition [3]pros, face to face engagement.*

The name, גבריאל *is very expressive: it is compounded word of* גבורה *geburah, a strong and valiant one, and* אל *el, [1]Gabriel - Elohim is my hero!)*

1:20 So you want a sign? You will be dumb and unable to say a word until these things happen! Unbelief doesn't have a voice in this matter!

1:21 And all the people were on tippy toe, wondering what Zechariah's delay in the temple could possibly be all about?

1:22 When he finally came out, he couldn't speak. They then realized that he encountered a vision in the inner sanctuary. He tried his best to explain with signs that he was unable to talk.

1:23 Thus he completed his term in the temple and returned home.

1:24 Elizabeth fell pregnant and hid herself for 5 months. *(In his, "Medical Language of Luke", Mr. Hobart says that the number of words referring to pregnancy, barrenness, etc., used by Luke, is almost as large as that used by Hippocrates. Compare Luk 1:31; Luk 1:24; Luk 2:5; Luk 1:7; Luk 20:28. All of these, except Luk 1:24,* **sunelaben,** *are* *peculiar to himself, and all, of course, in common use among medical writers.)*

1:25 She was thinking that by the time she is visibly pregnant, the testimony of this miracle would be of great significance and everyone would know that she is redeemed from the stigma of her barrenness. *(Her barren condition was a reflection of the condition of Israel - when will the promise of the Messiah be fulfilled! Has the prophetic word failed!?)*

1:26 By the time that Elizabeth was 6 months pregnant, the messenger Gabriel was commissioned by God to the town of Nazareth in Galilee.

1:27 Gabriel was to visit Mary, a ¹young, virgin girl, engaged to marry Joseph, a descendant of David. *(The word ¹parthenos, literally, "from Athens" - an epithet meaning "Virgin", applied by the Greeks to several goddesses, especially Athena. Always associated with a virgin girl - as in LXX Isa 7:14. [The LXX was the Jewish Scriptures of the time. The Septuagint, from the Latin: septuāgintā literally "seventy"; often abbreviated as 70 in Roman numerals, i.e., LXX; sometimes called the Greek Old Testament. It is the earliest extant Koine Greek translation of the Hebrew scriptures. [It was at the request of Ptolemy II Philadelphus (285–247 BCE) by 70 Jewish scholars or, according to later tradition, 72, with six scholars from each of the Twelve Tribes of Israel.] The discovery of the Qumran scrolls reveal that the LXX represents much older manuscripts than our OT, which used the 1000 years later Masoretic text.] In the MS text the word virgin was changed to, an unmarried girl.*

The most widely accepted view today is that the Septuagint provides a reasonably accurate record of an early Hebrew textual variant that differed from the ancestor of the Masoretic text as well as those of the Latin Vulgate, where both of the latter seem to have a more similar textual heritage. This view is supported by comparisons with Biblical texts found at the Essene settlement at Qumran [the Dead Sea Scrolls].)

1:28 Entering the house, he stood in front of her and greeted her with a most joyful salute! "Heavenly ¹bliss, in its most bountiful extreme is yours! The extravagant favor of God [for mankind] infuses you with grace! The ²Lord is with you!" *(The verb, κεχαριτωμενη, ¹kecharitoomene, is the Perfect Passive Participle of χαριτόω charitoō. It is only used here and repeated twice in Eph 1:6 See my comment in Luke 1:1 on the use of the Perfect Passive Participle.*

Then Gabriel reminds her of the prophetic word in Isa 7:14 by saying, ὁ Κύριος μετὰ σοῦ - **ho Kurios meta sou** - *the Lord is **with** you! Now the spoken language was Aramaic so what Mary heard was,* **²Immanuel!** *This immediately reminds of Isaiah 7:14!* **"Therefore the Lord himself will give you a sign: Behold, a virgin will be with child and bear a son, and she will call his name Immanuel -** עמנואל *Immanuel, **God with us**, with* עמ - `*im meaning, immediate, inseparable association; as in the Greek,* μετὰ **meta** - *with.*

The oldest MSS. do not have "Blessed are you among women" here, but in verse 42.)

1:29 She was deeply perplexed and reasoned within herself. Realizing the massive significance of this salutation! *(διαταράσσω diatarassō; greatly perplexed; διαλογίζομαι dialogizomai)*

1:30 The Messenger spoke to her and immediately re-assured her to have no fear - "God is head over heels in love with you! This is your moment to discover ¹how favored you have always been! *(Aorist active ¹ευρες.)*

1:31 For behold, you will be ¹mystically captured in your womb and conceive and bear a son. And you shall name him Jesus! *(The word, συλλαμβάνω ¹**sullambanō**, means to capture/arrest; thus to conceive - the male sperm is "captured" in the womb [en gastri]. Now, since the spoken language of the day was Aramaic, Gabriel obviously spoke Aramaic to Mary and instructed her, that the name of this wonder child is to be* יהושׁיע *Yehoshia, Jaweh rescued!*

Iēsoús is the Greek translation of the Hebrew/Aramaic word, יהושׁיע *Yehoshia, Jaweh rescued! This verb is the Hif'il 3rd person Past tense. Moses changed Joshua's name from* הושׁע *Hoshea, meaning "he rescued" - to* יהושׁע *Yehoshua - Yaweh rescued! In prophetic endorsement of God's salvation unveiled in Jesus. Numbers 13:16. These are the names of the men whom Moses sent to spy the land; and Moses called Hoshea [he saved] son of Nun, Yehoshua -* Ἰησοῦς *- Iēsous in the LXX Septuagint [H3091] See John 12:13.*

This name, combines with the powerful prophetic words of Gabriel's greeting, and reminds Mary of the virgin conception of עמנואל *Immanuel, as prophesied in Isaiah 7:14 in 700BC. This encounter reveals that the salvation of the human race from their "lost" identity and sense of separation from God, is realized in this child! Jesus is God Incarnate [en carne, in flesh], representing the entire human race in his person. This is the desire and resolve of God ,"God with us!"- it* is the boldest and grandest declaration of the essence of the gospel, God cannot be God without us! In the man, Jesus the Christ, mankind is fully included and represented and therefore, in the genius of God, rescued from every definition of distance and separation!

Both the full form Yehoshua and the abbreviated form Yeshua were in use during the Gospel period – and in relation to the same person, as in the Hebrew Bible references to Yehoshua/Yeshua son of Nun, and Yehoshua/Yeshua the high priest in the days of Ezra.

This conversation also connects most significantly with the prophetic word in Isaiah 9:6,7 For unto us a child is born, to us a son is given; and the government will be upon his shoulder, and his name will be called "Wonderful Counselor, Mighty God, Everlasting Father, Prince of Peace." Of the increase of his government and peace there will be no end, upon the throne of David, and over his kingdom, to establish it, and to uphold it with justice and with righteousness from this time forth and for evermore. The zeal of the LORD of hosts will do this.

The Apostolic bible's rendering, reads, "For a child has been born to us; a Son was given to us, of whom the sovereignty became upon his shoulders; and his name is called, Messenger of great counsel, wonderful, mighty God, potentate, ruler of peace, father of the Ages."

The coming One, who shall bruise the serpent's head, shall be the woman's "Seed"-the Son of woman, that so he may become more truly, the Son of Man; while later a strange expression finds its way into the sacred prophecy, how "a Virgin shall conceive, and bear a son." The Expositor's Bible Commentary.)

1:32 The eminence of his stature will be magnificent. He will be known as the son of the Most High. And the Lord God will ¹return to him what already belongs to him, the throne of his father David! (The word, ¹didomi, to give; also means to give to someone what already belongs to them, to return.)

1:33 And he will reign as king over the house of Jacob and his kingdom will be without any boundaries.

1:34 And Mary asked the Messenger, "So how can this be possible while I am still a virgin?"

1:35 And he said to her, "Holy Spirit will overwhelm you - hovering over you in the power of the Most High. Therefore, this holy begotten one will be called, son of God!

1:36 Oh, and let me tell you the good news about your aunt Elizabeth! She, who everyone called barren, is now already six months pregnant with a son, in her old age!"

1:37 Then Gabriel quotes Genesis 18:14 from the Septuagint, "Every word of God is equal to God's power and purpose to perform that word!" *(μὴ ἀδυνατεῖ παρὰ τῷ θεῷ παν ῥῆμα; me adunatei para too theo pan rhema, This immediately reminds Mary of God's conversation with Abraham when Sarah laughed in unbelief! And her laughter of unbelief was turned into laughter of delight!)*

1:38 Then Mary responded, "See, I am the handmaid of the Lord; I wish for it be with me exactly according to this conversation!" And with that, the messenger left.

1:39 And Mary arose and departed with urgent intent to the mountainous region of Judea. *(Arose [anastāsa] - Luke is very fond of this word; he uses it sixty times against the twenty-two times it is used in the rest of the N.T.*

Hebron, the chief city in the hill country, was also called, the city of the priests. Jos 21:11. It was situated within the tribe of Judah, about forty miles south of Jerusalem, and approximately eighty miles from Nazareth.

The name of the village near Hebron, where Zacharias lived, is Juttah. Josh 15:55. Robertson.)

1:40 She went directly to Zechariah's house and saluted Elizabeth!

1:41 When Elizabeth heard Mary's greeting, the baby leaped in her womb and Holy Spirit flooded her being.

1:42 Overwhelmed with joy she declared, [1]well spoken of and greatly celebrated are you in every woman's conversation! And greatly celebrated is he, the fruit of your womb! *(The word, eulogēmene, is the Perfect Passive Participle feminine and eulogēmenos, the masculine, from eulogeō to speak well of; to praise; to celebrate. The Perfect Passive Participle is a hebraistic equivalent for the superlative.)*

1:43 [1]What could be behind all of this? Whose idea is this, that I would I be so honored to have the mother of my Lord [2]visit me! *(The word, ποθεν [1]pothen, who or what is behind all this!? Literally have come all this way to [2]face me - pros - stand in front of me.)*

1:44 As soon as I heard the sound of your joyful greeting, the baby leapt within me with delight! *(The word, [1]agalliasisis is* *only used in the LXX and the New Testament - it means extreme exultation. From **agan** [much] and **hallomai** to jump with joy!)*

1:45 Oh, how supremely blessed is she who knew without a doubt that this [1]fantastic thing, which was told her [2]by the Lord, would fully unfold! *(The word, λελαλημενοις **lelalemenois** is the Perfect Passive Participle of λαλέω **laleō**, to speak. Again, the hebraistic equivalent for the [1]superlative. The preposition [2]**para**, indicates close proximity, a thing proceeding from a sphere of influence, with a suggestion of union of place of residence, to have sprung from its author and giver, originating from, denoting the point from which an action originates, intimate connection. Luke 1:38 Then Mary responded, "See, I am the handmaid of the Lord; I wish for it be with me exactly according to this conversation!")*

1:46 Then Mary responded, I extol the Lord with all my heart!

1:47 My spirit also [1]overflows with joy [2]in God my Savior! *(The word, ἀγαλλιάω **agalliaō**, means to be exceedingly glad; to rejoice greatly; from **agan** [much] and ἄλλομαι **hallomai**, to leap; to spring up, gush up like water from an artesian well. See my notes in Titus 3:6. Then, the words, τῷ Θεῷ τῷ σωτῆρί μου, **too theo, too sooteri mou**, are in the [2]Dative Case - indirect object, also location "in"; thus, in God my Savior.)*

1:48 I am so aware of God's favorable gaze upon my life - even though I am a handmaid of no prominent social standing - from now on, his favor will be endorsed in [1]every birth and his blessing will be evident for all [1]generations to realize! *(God's Favor is not a reward for good behavior or social status! Christ in the nations [**en ethnos**] is the mystery that was hidden for ages and generations but now unveiled in the incarnation revelation! His favor will be endorsed in [1]every birth - πασαι γενεαι **pasai geneai**. See also verse 50.)*

1:49 He has done great things for me - he is indeed the mighty one and his name is [1]extravagant goodness! *(Holy is his name - [1]speaking Aramaic, Mary most probably used the word חסד **chesed**, or **chasidutha**, which though we sometimes translate holy, yet the proper meaning is abundant goodness, exuberant kindness. Adam Clarke. The word is used of kindness or love between people, as well as of love or mercy and the generosity of God towards humanity.)*

1:50 The [1]kindness of God in the gift of life, [2]from birth to birth, is forever celebrated in awe! *(The word, ἔλεος [1]**eleos**, kindness,* *mercy, generosity, good will; a desire to help. The words, εἰς γενεὰς και γενεὰς [2]eis [3]geneas kai geneas, literally, from birth to birth. [generation to generation] eis - indicates a point reached in conclusion. To be overwhelmed with his mercy is to be awestruck with his generosity, every-time we witness the miracle of birth! The birth-theme is obviously most prominent in Mary's mind! The birth of the Savior will give context and significance to every birth on the planet! She symbolizes the dream of Elohim-incarnate, about to be redeemed and realized in every human life!)*

1:51 What he has accomplished in me, is by the strength of his arm. He confused the religious-philosophies of those who boasted in their puffed-up, home-made self-righteousness. *(Isa 52:10 The LORD has bared his holy arm before the eyes of all the nations; and all the ends of the earth shall see the salvation of our God. See John 12:38, Their persistent unbelief reminds of what Isaiah said, "Lord, who has believed our report? To whom has the arm of the Lord been revealed! [Isa 53:1.] Who understands how God has reached into our world? The incarnation is God's arm, reaching into our immediate moment! Also John 3:35 The theme of this conversation celebrates the extravagant love the Father has for the Son - and in him every gift of God is revealed - his hand extends God's touch; he is God's embrace of the human race!)*

1:52 In this rescuing act of God, he dethroned the ruling dynasties *[of the performance-based religious mindsets]* **and [1]elevated the [2]downtrodden on high!** *(The word, ὑψόω [1]hupsoō, to lift up on high, to exalt; to raise to the very summit of well-being, dignity, honor and happiness. Larry Richard writes, In Greek culture, [2]tapeinos and its derivatives were words of contempt. The Greeks saw man as the measure of all things. Thus, to be low on the social scale or to be socially powerless, was seen as shameful. Mary is moved by the realization that what has happened in her, was totally God's doing - it was entirely grace based - with no grounds for human effort or personal contribution to boast in. This is what puts religion out of business.)*

1:53 He feasted the famished with choice gifts and dismissed the rich, empty-handed.

1:54 [1]With his mind, inseparably focused on his mercy, he [2]embraced his child Israel to himself in mirror-association. *(The word, μνάομαι [1]mnaomai, to be mindful, to remember; through the idea of fixture in the mind; focus. The word ἀντιλαμβάνομαι [2]antilambanomai - from, anti, over against - thus, mirrored in. And*

24

λαμβάνω **lambanō** *to lay hold of, to take with the hand, to take what is one's own, to associate with one's self as companion.*)

1:55 Just as he has spoken face to face to our fathers, to Abraham and his seed concluding in this Age!

1:56 And Mary remained with Elizabeth for almost three months and then returned home.

1:57 Then Elizabeth's time to give birth was due and she had a son.

1:58 And her neighbors and relatives celebrated with her when they learned how magnificently the Lord had ¹magnified his mercy with her. *(He had ¹magnified his mercy. See 1 Samuel 12:24, Sept. ὅτι εἴδετε ἃ ἐμεγάλυνεν μεθ' ὑμῶν, a Hebrew expression, pointing to the generosity and goodness of God.)*

1:59 And on the eighth day they brought the child to be circumcised and be given the name of his father, Zechariah. *("Would have named" - ekaloun - Conative Imperfect Tense; they intended to name him Zechariah.)*

1:60 But his mother insisted that he should be named John.

1:61 They were surprised, since no-one in the family had that name.

1:62 And with sign language they asked Zechariah what name he wished to call his son.

1:63 He requested a writing tablet and wrote, his name is John. Everyone marvelled. *(Yochanan - יהוחנן Jaweh is gracious.)*

1:64 Then ¹suddenly, his mouth was opened and his tongue released and he spoke praises to God. *(The word, ¹parachrēma, immediately; is used nineteen times in the N.T., seventeen times by Luke [in this gospel and in Acts].)*

1:65 The entire neighborhood was filled with awe. This became the topic of conversation throughout the mountain region of Judea. *(The word, διελαλεῖτο **dielaleito** from διαλαλέω, means, continuous talk, back and forth between people; also a word only Luke uses.)*

1:66 And everyone who heard about this, treasured it in their hearts, wondering about the significance of this child's destiny. The hand of the Lord was clearly with him. *(The saying, "the* *hand of the Lord" - cheir Kuriou, is another expression that is unique in Luke's writing; see also my comment in Luke 1:51, Isaiah said, "Lord, who has believed our report? To whom has the arm of the Lord been revealed!" [Isa 53:1.] Who understands how God has reached into our world? The incarnation is God's arm, reaching into our immediate moment! His hand extends God's touch; he is God's embrace of the human race!)*

1:67 His father, Zechariah, filled with Holy Spirit, overflowed in prophetic utterance: *(Nearly every phrase is a direct quote from the Psalms and Prophets.)*

1:68 Praise the Lord, the God of Israel who rescued his people out of slavery, having never lost [1]sight of their plight. *(See Heb 2:6 for the use of episkeptomai, "Somewhere in the Scriptures it is written, 'What is it about the human species that God cannot get them out of his mind? What does he [1]see in the son of man, that so captivates his gaze?'" [The word [1]episkeptomai, from epi, continuous influence upon, and skopos, to view; to observe with keen interest.])*

1:69 He has raised up our strong Savior within the household of his child, David. *(The term, Horn of salvation [keras sōtērias], is a common metaphor in the O.T. See Psa 132:13 For the LORD has chosen Zion; he has desired it for his habitation. Ps 132:17 There I will make a horn to sprout for David; I have prepared a lamp for my anointed.)*

1:70 This has happened exactly as foretold by the prophets of old.

1:71 This means salvation from everything hostile to us; we are rescued out of the grip of everything contrary to us! *(The word, ἐχθρός echthros means, that which is hostile or contrary.)*

1:72 You have accomplished everything that your goodness and generosity proclaimed in your [1]sacred covenant with our fathers. *(The word translated holy, [1]hagios, from ἁγνός hagnos, exciting reverence, venerable, esteemed, sacred, pure, clean, immaculate, from the Hebrew, גח chag [pronounce the 'ch' as in Bach] to feast; a ceremonial festival; covenant meal.)*

1:73 As in the face to face oath which he gave to Abraham our father.

1:74 This was his resolve and gift to us all along - he undertook to rescue us out of the grip of everything contrary to us, freeing us to worship him without fear,

1:75 in [1]spontaneous innocence and righteousness, every day of our lives. *(The word, ὁσιότης hosiotēs suggests an innocence beyond the written code.)*

1:76 And you child, will be named the one who unveils the thoughts of the Most High; for you will go before the face of the Lord to prepare the way of the Lord; to turn our attention to a face to face encounter with his prophetic intention. *(See 1:17)*

1:77 And so, to [1]endue us with the knowledge of salvation, for everyone to become fully acquainted with their forgiveness and their release from bondage to the distortions of sin. *(The verb [1]δουναι is not the future of the verb didomi, to endue, to bestow a gift; it is the Aorist Infinitive where the thought is not the prophetic, but the necessity of the inevitable consequence as a result of something. Thus, this gift is a given, to begin with! The Aorist Infinitive indicates prior completion of an action in relationship to a point in time. Greek Infinitives could have either a Present or Aorist form. The contrast between the two forms was not necessarily one of time, it is a difference of aspect. The Present Infinitive was used to express progressive or imperfective aspect. It pictures the action expressed by the verb as being in progress. The Aorist Infinitive however does not express progressive aspect. It presents the action expressed by the verb as a completed unit with a beginning and end. Forgiveness is a non-negotiable!)*

1:78 The understanding of the tender affections and goodness of God is the conduit, sourced from on high, in which the dawn of his gaze will arise within us like the sun!

1:79 Those in darkness, snared in the fearful shadows of death, upon them light shone, to guide their feet on the smooth highway of peace. *(See Titus 3:4 Oh happy day! It was the generosity of God and his fondness for mankind that dawned on us like a shaft of light. Our days of darkness were over! Light shone everywhere and we became aware: God rescued the human race!*

Also Isa 9:2 The people who walk in darkness have seen a great light. The ones who dwell in the land of the shadow of death, on them, light shone.

To guide κατευθύναι from εὐθύς, straight; the removal of hindrances. See Isa 40:3-5 A voice cries: "In the wilderness prepare the way of the Lord, make straight in the desert a highway for our God. Every valley shall be lifted up, and every mountain and hill be made low; the crooked places shall be made straight, even the rough places shall be made smooth. And the glory of the LORD shall be revealed, and all flesh shall see it together, for the mouth of the LORD has spoken."

In the incarnate Christ, God removed every definition of distance; every possible excuse humanity could have to feel separated from God was removed once and for all.)

1:80 And the child grew and became strong in spirit, and was in the wilderness till the day of his public appearance before Israel. *(Notes on John the Baptist see John 1:19-36.)*

2:1 It was during that time when Caesar Augustus decreed a census to be taken throughout the Empire. *(Caesar Augustus was the first emperor of the Roman Empire, reigning for 41 years, from 27 BC until his death in AD 14. His birth name was Octavianus, meaning Eighth. [David was the eighth son of Jesse, See v 4.] Octavius was named in his maternal great-uncle, Julius Caesar's will as his adopted son and heir. He was proclaimed Augustus [honorable; distinguished] by the senate who appointed him as Emperor. He rejected monarchical titles, and instead called himself Princeps Civitatis - "First Citizen of the State".*

Robertson writes, No such decree was mentioned by Greek or Roman historians and it was for long assumed by many scholars that Luke was in error. But papyri and inscriptions have confirmed Luke on every point in these crucial verses Luk 2:1-7. See W.M. Ramsay's books - Was Christ Born at Bethlehem? Luke the Physician. The Bearing of Recent Discovery on the Trustworthiness of the N.T.)

2:2 This was the first Census of Quirinus, governor of Syria. *("Cyrenius," or "Quirinius," was not governor of Syria until 12 or 15 years after the birth of Jesus. Jesus was born during the reign of Herod. At that time "Varus" was president of Syria. According to Dr. Lardner, the passage here is called the "first" to distinguish it from one "afterward" taken by Cyrenius, Act 5:37. It is said to be the census taken by "Cyrenius; governor of Syria; "not that he was "then" governor, but that it was taken by him who was afterward familiarly known as governor. "Cyrenius, governor of Syria," was the name by which the man was known when Luke wrote his gospel. Albert Barnes.)*

2:3 Each journeyed to the town where their family register was kept.

2:4 Joseph also, being of the lineage of David, travelled up from Nazareth in Galilee to Judea; he had to register in Bethlehem where David was born. *(Micah 5:2 And you, Bethlehem Ephrathah, [בית לחם house of bread; אפרתה place of fruitfulness;] the least among the families of Judah, out of you one will come to me who is to be ruler in Israel; whose going out has been purposed from time past, from the eternal days. 1 Sam 17:12 Now David was the eighth son of an Ephrathite of Bethlehem in Judah, named Jesse. The number 8 is the number for new beginnings, resurrection and regeneration. Through gematria, by counting the letter values of the Greek transliteration of Jesus' name, amounts to 888.*

See Isa 11:1 Then a shoot will come out from the stump of Jesse, and a branch from its roots will bear fruit. See notes on Jesse in Luke 3:32 Son of **Jesse** ישי Jaweh is my husband - from יאיש from יֶש yêsh/yaysh. From an unused root meaning to stand out, or exist; entity; used adverbially or as a copula for the substantive verb היה **hâyâh** H1961 to breathe; to be; to exist; from the core of the name of Jaweh, יהוה "existing". Thus, the root word for Jesse, היה **hajah**, in the Ancient Hebrew is, - the pictograph represents one who is looking at a great sight with his hands raised. In David's father, Jesse, it is the one looking at the other in mirror likeness! See Act 13:22, Rom 15:12, And further Isaiah says, "The root of Jesse shall come, he who rises to rule the Gentiles; in him shall the Gentiles hope."

Also, hidden in the name Jesse is the prophetic picture of the incarnation - Jaweh embracing man! The word for man, איש **ish** and woman, adding the ה breath-sound, hey, **ishah** אשה - Thus, Jesse also includes the jod connecting Jaweh with **ish**, man - Jaweh, the incarnate man!)

2:5 Together with his ¹wife Mary, who was already ²well advanced in her pregnancy. (His ¹betrothed, εμνηστευμενη **emnesteumene** - See Math 1:24 "When Joseph woke up, he did what the angel of the Lord had commanded him to do. He took Mary to be his wife." The word, ἐγκύῳ ²**enkuo**, en, in and κύω **kuō**, to swell [with young], that is, bend, curve; a billow [as bursting or toppling] Again a unique word in the NT only used by Dr Luke.)

2:6 And there in Bethlehem her time was fulfilled.

2:7 And she gave birth to her first-born son, and wrapped him in strips of cloth and laid him down in a feeding-trough, since there was no room for them in the inn.

2:8 Now there were also shepherds in that area keeping watch at night over their flock, in the open fields. (Note the singular use of the word, τὴν ποίμνην αὐτῶν **ten poimnen autoon**, their flock, the temple-flock, specially devoted to sacrifice. The Shepherds were raising sheep to be without blemish for sacrifice. Jerusalem's economic heart was the Holy Temple, the only place where Israelites could sacrifice animals as offerings to God.)

2:9 Then suddenly a celestial shepherd messenger of the Lord stood by them and the light of the glory of the Lord engulfed them. They were petrified.

2:10 The celestial messenger immediately calmed them and said, "You have no reason to fear! Listen! I have the most wonderful announcement to make - this will lead to the great encounter of the most joyful bliss for every single person on the planet!

2:11 For your [1]**Savior was born this day in the city of David, the Messiah, the Master.** *(¹Σωτηρ, to make safe, to deliver, preserve, to make alive, thus used by the Septuagint for* היחה *hecheiah, to cause to escape; also for* טלפ *thalaph to confide in, to hope. Adam Clarke.*

He is the Christ, ὁ Χριστος, ho Christos, the anointed. The word, chrestos, kind, benevolent, from xeir, hand which is also connected to the word xristos, from χριω to anoint. To draw the hand over, to anoint, to measure; see also the Hebrew for Messiah, משיח *to anoint, from mashach,* משח *to draw the hand over, to measure! [Analytical Hebrew and Chaldee Lexicon, B Davidson.]*

LXX Isa 9:5 [:6 in our Bibles] ὅτι παιδιον ἐγεννήθη ἡμῖν, υἱὸς καὶ ἐδόθη ἡμῖν.

Isa 9:5 כי־ילד ילד לנו בן נתן *ki yeled yâlad a child is born, to us lanu a son is given ben nathan.*

For unto us a child is born,.... This is a reason of all that is said in the context; of the great light that shone upon and was seen by those that sat in darkness, and in the land of the shadow of death; of the great joy among the people; of the breaking off of the yoke, rod, and staff of the oppressor; and of the burning of garments rolled in blood, so putting an end to war, and establishing peace; all which is owing to the child here said to be born... John Gill.

Isa 9:2 The people who walked in darkness have seen a great light; those who dwelt in a land of deep darkness, on them has light shined.

Isa 9:3 Thou hast multiplied the nation, thou hast increased its joy; they rejoice before you as with joy at the harvest, as men rejoice when they divide the spoil.

Isa 9:4 For the yoke of his burden, and the staff for his shoulder, the rod of his oppressor, thou hast broken as on the day of Midian.

Isa 9:7 Of the increase of his government and of peace there will be no end, upon the throne of David, and over his kingdom, to establish it, and to uphold it with justice and with righteousness from this time forth and for evermore. The zeal of the LORD of hosts will do this.)

2:12 This is how you will know it's him, you'll find a little baby, wrapped in strips of cloth and lying in a feeding-trough!

2:13 The next moment, a heavenly host of multitudes of celestial messengers joined and erupted in accolades of praise telling the God-story! *(The word, αἰνέω aineō a story of tribute and honor.)*

2:14 God's highest and grandest [1]intention in the heavens is [2]dove-tailed upon earth in unbroken, incarnate oneness; in being human, he exibits [3]his delight with mankind! *(The word, doxa, often translated, glory, means opinion or, intention. Peace, εἰρήνη [2]eirēnē from εἴρω eirō - to join, as in carpentry, a dove-tail joint. Then follows, en anthrōpois eudokias. It is not, "Peace to all men and women on earth who please him"; as if God's delight is only a reward for those who qualify. He loved us when we were at our worst. And he loved us first! The Genitive, [3]eudokias is undoubtedly correct, supported by the oldest and best uncials. [Aleph, A B D W] Thus, mankind is God's delight! See, Colossians 1:19 God is fully at home in him. Jesus exhibits God's happy delight to be human. [Delightful intent, eudokeo.])*

2:15 Then, as the celestial heralds withdrew into the heavens, the shepherds immediately determined to go to Bethlehem and witness with their own eyes, the prophetic word which has now come to pass, as they have learned from the Lord.

2:16 They departed with great urgency and searched until they found the trophy - Mary and Joseph with their little baby, who was lying in a feeding-trough.

2:17 Having now seen for themselves, they boldly shared the significance of their encounter and how the prophetic word was communicated to them concerning this child. *(These shepherds, having charge of flocks devoted to sacrifice, would presently be in the temple, and would meet those who came to worship and to sacrifice, and so they proclaimed the Messiah to them. Vincent.)*

2:18 Everyone who heard their story, was filled with wonder!

2:19 Mary treasured all these sayings, pondering them in her heart; and so forming, as in a mental mosaic, her picture of the Christ, who was to be. *(The words, suntereo, to treasure together, in the Imperfect Active Tense, thus, treasuring these things all along and pondering, sumballo, the Present Participle, putting them together. And so, in later years, we read [Luke 2:51] how "His mother kept all these sayings in her heart," gathering up the thoughts and fragmentary sentences.)*

2:20 The shepherds returned, celebrating the marvelous events and filled to overflowing with the God-story that unfolded before their eyes! *(It is a historic fact that there was a tower near Bethlehem, called Eder, or "the Tower of the Flock," around which were pastured the flocks destined for the Temple sacrifice.)*

2:21 On the eighth day the child was circumcised and named Jesus; just as the celestial messenger told Mary before he was conceived.

2:22 When the forty days of cleansing were completed, according to the instructions of Moses, they went up to Jerusalem to present the boy to the Lord. *(The mother of a child was Levitically unclean for forty days after the birth of a son - The first-born son of every household was to be redeemed of the priest at the price of five shekels, as a memorial of Israel's deliverance out of slavery. Exodus 13:2-12. Here, the boy Jesus is himself the fulfillment of the prophetic picture of mankind's deliverance from slavery.)*

2:23 Just as it was written in the law, every boy that opens the womb shall be called holy to the Lord. *(Luke mentions the law five times in this chapter [more than in the entire book] - obviously inspired by his travel companion, Paul. See Gal 4:4, But then the day dawned; the most complete culmination of time! [Everything predicted, was concluded in Christ!] The Son arrived, commissioned by the Father; his legal passport to the planet was his mother's womb. In a human body exactly like ours he lived his life subject to the same scrutiny of the law. Gal 4:5 His mandate was to rescue the human race from the regime of the law of performance and announce the revelation of their true sonship, redeemed in God.)*

2:24 They were then to offer a sacrifice just as the law of the Lord said, a pair of turtle doves or two nestlings. *(For those who could not afford a lamb, two turtle doves or two dove-chicks would suffice. Lev 12:8 The idea of the sacrifice was, that the youngest possible animal symbolized innocence most perfectly. Doves also, were symbolic of innocence.)*

2:25 And significantly so, there happened to be a man Simeon, in Jerusalem; he was a righteous man who embraced the goodness of God. *(The name, Simeon, in Aramaic, שמעון shim'ôn - means, one who heard. The word εὐλαβής eulabēs, one who embraces/grasps goodness. This is again unique to Luke - he alone uses this word here, then twice in the book of Acts. The noun, εὐλάβεια eulabeia occurs twice in Hebrews - See Heb 5:7 When he faced the horror of his imminent death, he presented his urgent plea to God in an outburst of agonizing emotion and with tears.)*

33

He prayed with urgent intent to be delivered from death, knowing God's power was saving him and that he enjoyed God's full attention - he had a firm grip on the prophetic word. [Not because he feared, as some translations have put it, but because he fully grasped that he was the fulfillment of Scripture; he knew that he would be raised on the third day; [Hosea 6:2] eu + lambano - he had a firm grip; he fully realized the significance of his mission.])

2:26 Simeon had a Holy Spirit encounter and knew that he would not die before he sees the Lord's Anointed.

2:27 Prompted in the spirit, he arrived at the temple as the parents of the child Jesus, brought him in, as prescribed in their tradition and law.

2:28 And Simeon, holding the little child in his arms began to speak eloquent praises to God and said,

2:29 My Master, I am fully satisfied; you can now release your bond-servant in peace. I am holding your incarnate word in my arms!

2:30 And my eyes have seen your salvation! *(See Gen 49:18 For I waited for your salvation o Lord!)*

2:31 The very salvation which [1]prophetically and perfectly [2]mirrors your face in [3]every individual human life! *(The word, ἑτοιμάζω [1]hetoimazō is drawn from the oriental custom of sending on before kings on their journeys persons to level the roads and make them passable - see Isa 40:3-5 A voice cries: "In the wilderness prepare the way of the Lord, make straight in the desert a highway for our God. Every valley shall be lifted up, and every mountain and hill be made low; every crooked place shall be made straight, and the rough places smooth. And the glory of the Lord shall be revealed, and all flesh shall see it together, for the mouth of the Lord has spoken.*

I have taken the mirror idea from the word, πρόσωπον [2]prosōpon, face to face. Note the words, πάντων τῶν λαῶν, [3]pantoon toon laoon, where the noun is plural, all the peoples, and refers equally to the Gentiles. These words are in the Genitive case, thus, this salvation belongs to the entire human race!

See Marvin Vincent's Introduction to his Word Studies in Luke [Kindle] on Luke's universal gospel.)

2:32 A light [1]concluding in the ultimate unveiling of the Gentiles as well as the glory of his people Israel. *(The preposition [1]eis*

indicates a point reached in conclusion; the ultimate. [And the glory of the Lord shall be revealed, and all flesh shall see it together. Isa 40:5.] See Paul's teaching on Israel and the Gentiles in Romans chapter 11. Rom 11:25 Do not be ignorant then of the mystery of their temporal exclusion; their blindness opened your eyes to the fullness of God's plan for the whole world. Rom 11:26 Once the nations realize the full extent of their inclusion, then all Israel shall also be saved. Just as it is written prophetically, "There shall come a Deliverer out of Zion; he shall turn ungodliness away from Jacob. Rom 11:32 In God's calculation the mass of mankind is trapped in unbelief. This qualifies all mankind for his mercy.

Also 2 Cor 4:6 The light source is founded in the same God who said, "Light, be!" And light shone out of darkness! He lit the lamp in our understanding so that we may clearly recognize the features of his likeness in the face of Jesus Christ reflected within us. 2 Cor 4:7 And now, in the glow of this glorious light and with unveiled faces we discover this treasure where it was hidden all along, in these frail skin-suits made of clay. Also 2 Cor 3:18 And we all, with new understanding, see ourselves in him as in a mirror. The days of window-shopping are over! In him every face is unveiled. In gazing with wonder at the blueprint of God displayed in human form, we suddenly realize that we are looking into a mirror, where every feature of his image articulated in Christ is reflected within us! The Spirit of the Lord engineers this radical transformation; we are led from an inferior mind-set to the revealed endorsement of our authentic identity. [From glory to glory, the glory of the flesh, which is the veiled, fading kind represented by Moses and the unfading, unveiled glory of God's image and likeness, mirrored in the face of Christ and now redeemed in us.])

2:33 And his Father and mother were awed by everything that was said about him.

2:34 And Simeon celebrated them and said to his mother Mary, know that this child will be laid down for the destruction and resurrection again of Israel's ¹multitudes. This will be a symbolic sign of controversy, ²ultimately mirroring the genius of God! (Simeon is not saying that some will fall and some will be raised - he speaks about the falling and the rising of the same people. Paul also uses the word, ¹**polus**, multitudes, in the same context in Rom 5:14-21. Again the preposition **eis**, points to the conclusion of something. The word **antilegomenon**, in the sentence, καὶ εἰς σημεῖον ἀντιλεγόμενον, a symbolic sign of controversy, I have also translated, mirroring, as in this conversation, the one stands **anti**,

35

or over against the other. This is the genius of God! In his life, death, decent into hell and his triumphant resurrection, Jesus mirrors 'you'-manity. As in 2 Cor 5:14 One has died for all; therefore all died! And Ephesians 2:5, while we were dead in our trespasses and sins, God co-quickened us and co-raised us and co-seated us together with Christ in heavenly places!

The fact that Jesus brought closure to a redundant sacrificial system is obviously a huge point of controversy to the Jewish mindset, but hidden in the mystery that none of the rulers of the world system understood, was the genius of God, whereby principalities were disarmed and rendered powerless to judge or condemn the human race! He was handed over for our sins, but raised for our innocence! Col 2:14,15.)

2:35 And a [1]sword shall also pierce your own soul, then the reasonings, dialogues and doubtful disputes of multitudes of hearts will be [2]uncovered. *(Having encountered the dramatic, prophetic word fulfilled in the divine conception of Immanuel, Mary then witnessed the priest perform the circumcision with a sharp knife on her darling baby when he was a mere 8 days old, which must have been so painful to her mother's heart. She would witness the many rumors and controversies around Jesus' conception, his life, ministry and eventual cruel trial and brutal crucifixion where his side was finally pierced with a spear! Luke reminds us in verse 51 that she pondered all these sayings in her heart. Yet, there were times when, even she and Jesus' siblings had their own reasonings and doubts. See Math 12:46-49. Also John 7:5.*

The word, [1]rhomphaia a large, long sword; This word is used 6 times in Revelation, Rev 1:16, Rev 2:12, Rev 2:16, Rev 6:8, Rev 19:15, Rev 19:21 - in the LXX [Greek Septuagint] it is used for the sword of the Lord. It is an exaggerated size to emphasise its symbolic use, pointing to the prophetic, incarnate Word that would pierce the veiled hearts of the masses and bring to light the revelation of the mystery of Christ in them!

See Heb 4:12 The message God spoke to us in Christ, is the most life giving and dynamic influence in us, cutting like a surgeon's scalpel, sharper than a soldier's sword, piercing to the deepest core of human conscience, to the dividing of soul and spirit; ending the dominance of the sense realm and its neutralizing effect upon the human spirit. In this way a person's spirit is freed to become the ruling influence again in the thoughts and intentions of their heart. The scrutiny of this living Sword-Logos detects every possible disease, discerning the body's deepest secrets where joint and bone-marrow meet. (The moment we cease from our own efforts to justify ourselves, by yielding to the integrity of the message that announces the genius and success of the Cross, God's word is triggered into action. What God spoke to us in sonship [the incarnation], radiates his image and likeness in our redeemed innocence. [Heb 1:1-3] This word powerfully penetrates and impacts our whole being; body, soul and spirit. Psa 139:2, You know the deepest impulse of my thoughts; engaging the secret longings of the heart!)

Heb 4:13 The entire person is thoroughly exposed to his scrutinizing gaze.

The Sword would always point back to mankind's original identity. The Hebrew word in Gen 3:24, הפך hâpak is a primitive root; meaning to turn about; by implication to change, to return, to be converted, turn back. Also in the Septuagint the same thought is communicated in the Greek word, strephō, which is the strengthened from the base of tropay; to turn around or reverse: - convert, turn again, back again, to turn self about. In Luke 15 the prodigal son returns to himself - Plato is quoted by Ackerman [Christian Element in Plato] as thinking of redemption as coming to oneself! See Notes on the splendor of the Gates Rev 21.

The word, ὅπως hopōs, points to the intention to take off the cover [ἀποκαλύπτω ²apokaluptō] of the multitudes [πολλός polus] of [διαλογισμοὶ dialogismoi] doubtful disputes and reasonings!)

2:36 There was also a prophetess Anna, the daughter of Phanuel, from the tribe of Asher. She was already far advanced in her days and a widow for eighty four years. Her husband died when she was only twenty one and married for seven years. *(She lived her ¹name! Her face was constantly turned upward- engaging her ²father's eyes! The ³happy family! The word, ¹ana, means upward; her ²father's name was Phanuel פְּנוּאֵל which means, the face of God and their tribe, Ashar אָשֵׁר - means happy! "She lived with her husband seven years since her virginity." This suggests she was 14 when married, then widowed at 21; now 84 years later, she is 105 years old! In Deuteronomy, Moses prophesies that for the tribe of Asher, Anna's tribe, "your strength will equal your days" Deut 33:25.)*

2:37 For all these years, since her husband's death, she ministered to the Lord continually in the temple with prayers and frequent fastings.

2:38 As Simeon concluded his prophetic song over the family, Anna ¹mirror-echoed his words in a song of thanksgiving to

God for the child. And from that day on, she told everyone in Jerusalem that their [1]Darling, the anticipated Messiah-redeemer has come! *(The word, ανθωμολογειτο anthomologeito, from anti, over against as in a mirror reflection and homologeo, to say the same thing; to mutually agree. The word, προσδέχομαι [1]prosdechomai, to receive someone in intimate companionship. Here, a Present, Passive, Participle in the Dative Case to have been embraced in companionship.)*

2:39 So, when the presentation in the temple and the relative ceremonies were concluded, the family returned to Galilee.

2:40 The child grew up to be a healthy, vigorous little boy, with an uncluttered mind full of [1]wisdom - living aware of the [2]constant influence of God's favor upon him. *(The word, [1]sophos, means wisdom, from saphes, clear. The preposition [2]epi, suggests a continual influence upon.)*

2:41 Every year his parents would journey to Jerusalem to celebrate the Pascha Feast. *(The word "passover" did not even exist before William Tyndale coined it for his Version of 1526-31. Previously the Hebrew and Greek were left untranslated. Passover, or Pasach, פסח protecting and rescuing. From an Arabic root which means to expand; to save. In Ancient Hebrew it is, ☐⧖⬭ [reading from right to left, the letter פ pe ⬭ means mouth; then the letter, ש or ס "s", which means thorn, ⧖ - this letter also has the meaning of a shield as thorn bushes were used by the shepherd to build a wall or shield to enclose his flock during the night to protect them from predators. Then, the letter, ☐ for the letter ch, like in the sound, ch in the word, Bach - it is a picture of a tent wall, to protect the occupants from the elements outside. Thus, the mouth speaking the prophetic word, announcing the good news of salvation from every possible threat.*

Jesus remains focussed on the mission of his life! In the scandalous genius of God, the slain and risen Lamb is the central theme of the book of Revelation. "Look! The Lion has conquered! He who is of the tribe of Judah, the root of David is qualified to open the scroll and its seven seals!" So I looked to see the Lion and there, as if fused into one with the throne and in unison with the four Living Beings, taking center stage in the midst of the elders, I saw a little Lamb, alive and standing; even though it appeared to have been violently butchered in sacrifice! It had seven horns and seven eyes, which are the seven Spirits of God, sent out to accomplish his bidding in all the earth. Rev 5:5,6. Also Zechariah 3:9 For behold, upon the stone which I have set before Joshua, upon a single stone with seven facets [eyes], I will engrave its inscription, says the LORD of hosts, I will remove the guilt of the earth in a single day.)

2:42 Now, when Jesus was twelve years old, they again went up to Jerusalem for the feast. *(See this most significant connection with Jesus' visit 18 years later, at the beginning of his ministry:*

John 2:13 Jesus then went up to Jerusalem in time for the Jewish Passover.

John 2:14 When he went into the temple he was shocked to find scores of traders selling their sacrificial items, cattle, sheep and doves. Even their money brokers were comfortably set up in the sanctuary. (The business of sin-consciousness has taken over the mindset of religion - until Jesus arrives.)

John 2:15 Then with a whip that he plaited of small ¹strands, he drove everyone with their sheep and oxen out of the temple and overturned the tables of the money brokers so that their money went flying all over the place. (Jesus dramatically reveals that his Father has no delight in our religious sacrificial systems and its sin-conscious currencies. ¹σχοῖνος - schoinos perhaps from skenos, tabernacle or skin - leather thongs - a profound prophetic picture of his own broken skin that would become the whip to drive out sin-consciousness from our minds - the ultimate cleansing of the temple - the sanctuary of God within us! See 1 Peter 1:18,19.)

John 2:16 He also drove the dove traders out with, "How dare you turn my Father's house into a shopping mall?" (See Luke 2:24.)

John 2:17 This incident reminded his disciples of the Scripture, "I am consumed with zeal for my Father's house!" (Psalm 69:9. God is ablaze with zeal for you! You are the temple of God - his address - his dwelling!)

John 2:18 The Jews demanded to know from Jesus how, what he has just done in the temple, could possibly point to the significance of his Messianic mission. "Show us a sign!"

John 2:19 To which Jesus responded, "The temple will be completely demolished by you and in three days I will raise it up!" (The word ¹lu-sate, to undo, demolish, is in the Aorist, Passive, imperative case; the distinction between the Aorist Imperative and the Present Imperative is one of aspect, not necessarily tense. Thus, to get something over and done with!

See Matthew 12:39,40 But he answered them, "An evil and adulterous generation seeks for a sign; but no sign shall be given to it except the sign of the Prophet Jonah. For as Jonah was three days and three nights in the belly of the whale, so will the son of man be three days and three nights in the heart of the earth.

"Ask a sign of the LORD your God; let it be deep as Sheol or high as heaven. But you would not, therefore the Lord himself will give you a sign. Behold, a virgin shall conceive and bear a son, and shall call his name Immanuel." Isaiah 7:11-14. "For unto us a child is born, to us a son is given; and the government will be upon his shoulder, and his name will be called Wonderful Counselor, Mighty God, Everlasting Father, Prince of Peace. Of the increase of his government and of peace there will be no end." Isaiah 9:6,7.

In his resurrection on the third day, God would co-quicken the human race and co-raise us together with him! Hosea 6:2, Ephesians 2:5. Human life will again be the tabernacle of God! "On the third day Esther put on her royal robes and stood in the inner court of the king's palace, opposite the king's hall. The king was sitting on his royal throne inside the palace opposite the entrance to the palace; and when the king saw Queen Esther standing in the court, she found favor in his sight and he held out to Esther the golden sceptre that was in his hand. Then Esther approached and touched the top of the sceptre." Esther 5:1,2

"And beginning with Moses and all the Prophets, he interpreted to them in all the Scriptures the things concerning himself." Luke 24:27 "They said to each other, did not our hearts ignite within us while he talked to us on the road, while he opened to us the Scriptures?" Luke 24:32 "Then he said to them, these are my words which I spoke to you, while I was still with you, that everything written about me in the law of Moses and the Prophets and the Psalms must be fulfilled. Then he opened their minds to understand the Scriptures, and said to them, Thus it is written, that the Christ should suffer and on the third day rise from the dead" Luke 24:44-46; See also Psalm 22 and Isaiah 53.

Matthew 16:21 From that time Jesus began to show his disciples that he must go to Jerusalem and suffer many things from the elders and chief priests and law professors, and be killed, and on the third day be raised.)

John 2:20 *The Jews responded with, "This temple was under construction for forty six years and you will rebuild it in just three days? Haha!"*

John 2:21 They did not understand that the temple Jesus was pointing to, was the human body. (In him, the only true address of God was to be redeemed in human life in his resurrection! See Hosea 6:2 "After two days he will revive us, on the third day he will raise us up!" Also Ephesians 2:5 and 1 Peter 1:3; Acts 7:47-50 But it was Solomon who built a house for him. Yet the Most High does not dwell in houses made with hands; as the Prophet says, 'heaven is my throne, and earth my footstool. What house will you build for me, says the Lord, or what is the place of my rest? Did not my hand make all these things?'

*The word **hieros** speaks of the greater temple building with all its outer courts etc. whereas the word Jesus uses here is **naos**, referring to the inner sanctuary - this is also the word Paul uses in 1 Corinthians 6:19 "Do you not realize that your body by design is the sacred shrine of the Spirit of God!" This is the most sacred place in the universe! There is nowhere in eternity that can match this! See John 1:14 "And the Word became flesh and now resides within us! And John 14:20 In that day you will know that I am in my Father and you in me and I in you!")*

John 2:22 These words of Jesus as well as their significant prophetic connection with Scripture gave such clear context to the disciples when they later, after his resurrection, recalled all these things.

John 2:23 Now during the Passover feast in Jerusalem, many believed in his Name - surely the signs he did confirmed his mission as the Messiah-Savior of the world?)

2:43 Having completed the Passover days, the parents went home without realising that their boy, Jesus, stayed behind in Jerusalem. *(In Luk 2:40 it was "the child " to **paidion**, here it is "the boy" **ho pais**, no longer the diminutive form.)*

2:44 Supposing him to be present in the group, they continued their journey and only began looking for him at the end of the first day. They frantically searched for him among their family and friends. *(The women usually went ahead and the men followed. Joseph may have thought Jesus was with Mary and Mary that he was with Joseph. "The Nazareth caravan was so long that it took a whole day to look through it" Plummer.)*

2:45 Finally when they realized that he was not anywhere in the group, they returned to Jerusalem on a mission to find him.

2:46 Back in Jerusalem they found him on the third day, sitting in the temple surrounded by teachers, *[Rabbis and members of the Temple-Sanhedrin],* **engaging their attention**

with remarkable questions. *(Twenty-one years later there would be another Easter where he disappears and is found again on the third day!)*

2:47 Everyone listening to him, was [1]**awed with wonder at his fantastic** [2]**insight into the entire prophetic thought! He responded with such genius to their questions; it was like he wrote the script!** *(The word, ἐξίστημι* [1]*existēmi, to be out of one's mind with wonder, to be besides one's self with amazement. The word, σύνεσις* [2]*sunesis, from συνίημι suniēmi - sun + eimi, together with my "I am-ness", to resonate; which means a flowing together as of two streams - a seamless merging, a fusion of thought. It suggests the grasp and comprehension that happens from comparing and combining things. A word only Paul uses and here Luke and another disciple of Paul, Mark who uses it in Mark 12:33, "To love him with all your heart, with all your **understanding**, with all your strength, and to love your neighbor as you love yourself; this is more important than all the burnt offerings and sacrifices."*

*Here is the same word in the LXX; see **Isa 52:13** in the Septuagint, "Behold! My boy shall be full of **understanding**; he shall be exalted and decorated with exceedingly great esteem." Ἰδοὺ Idou - "Behold! [συνήσει suniesei from suniemi, to understand; as in two rivers flowing together! Also carrying in it the idea of the Incarnation - the word made flesh - "In the Scriptures it is written about me!" My boy shall be full of understanding; [ὁ παῖς μου ho pais mou - my boy - kai hupsothesetai] he shall be exalted [kai doxasthesetai sphorda,] and decorated with exceeding great esteem." Note the LXX reads, my boy and not "servant" which is only in Masoretic Hebrew text. The MSS dates a thousand years later than the LXX.*

***Isa 52:14** As many were astonished at him—his appearance was so marred, beyond human semblance, and his form beyond that of the sons of men— **Isa 52:15** so shall he startle many nations; kings shall shut their mouths because of him; for that which has not been told them they shall see, and that which they have not heard they shall understand.*

*Also **LXX Ps 46:8**. [Ps 47:7 in the Masoretic text.] "He is the King over all the earth - sing psalms to him with understanding!" Again the word, συνετός sunetos, to mentally join together - to make sense - to put the pieces of the puzzle together!*

Then Luke uses the word, ἀπόκρισις apokrisis, from apo, away from and krino, to separate, put asunder, to pick out, select, choose, to approve, esteem, to prefer, to be of opinion, deem, to determine, resolve, decree, to judge, to dispute, to scrutinize in a forensic sense; thus, to respond with such genius that the matter is put beyond dispute. The word apokrisis is only used twice by Luke, and twice by John; See Luke 20:26, "And marvelling at his answer, they were silent.")

2:48 They were startled to see him in the temple. His mother scolded, "Son, how could you do this to us! Look at us; we are distraught at the thought that you could be dead! Oh how foolish of you to cause us such [1]agonizing grief! Everyone's been [2]frantically searching for you for three days!" *(We are grieving - ὀδυνάω [1]odunaō, to grieve; to be in sorrow, be in anguish, be tormented. The word, [2]ezētoumen is the Imperfect tense, describing the long drawn out search for three days.)*

2:49 He was surprised at their anxiety and said, "Why this desperate searching for me when you should know by now [1]what I am all about! I am about my Father's business. My Father defines my being and destiny!" *(The words, οὐκ ἤδειτε ὅτι ἐν τοῖς τοῦ πατρός μου δεῖ εἶναί με; Literally, "Did you not realize that I am destined to be who I am [ἐν τοῖς en tois] - in the all inclusive conversation and interest - of my Father!" [I am everything the prophets pointed to! Humanity is my Father's Real Estate!]*

Jesus is surprised that his parents' divine encounter of his conception and the amazing events around his birth, with all the prophetic happenings at the temple and the marvellous announcements of Simeon and Anna seem to be forgotten so soon! I'm on a rescue mission, remember! I am here to redeem the tabernacle of God - human life is my Father's residence! The things of my father's house consume me! [See my commentary on Luke 2:42. Also John 2:19 & Math 26:59-64.])

2:50 Sadly, they again seemed [1]unable to make the vital connection and thus failed to comprehend the significance of these words! *(Again Luke uses the word, οὐ συνῆκαν [1]ou sunekan, not connecting the dots! From suniemi, to join, or sync together in order to form a mental picture.)*

2:51 He [1]seamlessly engaged with them in his "earth-suit" and went down with them to Nazareth where he lived with them in submission to their parental expectations. All along his mother deeply treasured all these words and encounters in her heart. *(καὶ κατέβη μετ᾽ αὐτῶν - The word, καταβαίνω [1]katabainō, means to descend, as of celestial beings coming down to earth. In his fulfilling the* *prophetic word, having seamlessly stepped into their world as the incarnate son of man, he thus readily submitted himself to their parenthood and expectations. Without any compromize, the son of God is also naturally and fully the son of man. See Math 13:55 Is not this the carpenter's son? Is not his mother called Mary? And are not his brothers, James, Joseph, Simon and Jude?*

Phil 2:6 His being God's equal in form and likeness was official; his Sonship did not steal the limelight from his Father! Neither did his humanity distract from the deity of God!

Phil 2:7 His mission however, was not to prove his deity, but to embrace our humanity. Emptied of his reputation as God, he fully embraced our physical human form; born in our resemblance he identified himself as the servant of the human race. His love enslaved him to us!

Phil 2:8 And so we have the drama of the cross in context: the man Jesus Christ who is fully God, becomes fully man to the extent of willingly dying mankind's death at the hands of his own creation. He embraced the curse and shame of the lowest kind in dying a criminal's death. (Thus, through the doorway of mankind's death, he descended into our hellish darkness. Rev 9:1 and Eph 4:8-10.))

2:52 Meanwhile Jesus [1]continued to engage and advance with courageous progress in all things; in wisdom, in stature and in the consciousness of favor before God and his fellow human beings. *(The word, προκόπτω [1]**prokoptō** means, the progressive advance, as in cutting one's way through a jungle. It is used here in the Imperfect Active tense, προεκοπτεν, he continued to pioneer his way as the incarnate image bearer of the invisible God in human life. John 14:9, Col 1:15.)*

Notes on the Hebrew Alphabet

Notes on the Hebrew Alphabet

With the Babylonian exile, 586 BC, the Jews gradually stopped using the Paleo-Hebrew script, based on ancient pictographic letters, otherwise known as the Phoenician alphabet and instead adopted a square letter form of the Aramaic alphabet.

For the origin of the Phoenician alphabet, see this link to the Proto-Sinaitic Script,

https://en.wikipedia.org/wiki/Proto-Sinaitic_script

The Hebrew alphabet contains 22 letters and read from right to left.

א ב ג ד ה ו ז ח ט י כ ל מ נ ס ע פ צ ק ר ש ת

א Aleph ב Beth ג Gimel ד Daleth ה Hei ו Waw ז Zayin ח Chet ט Teth י Iod כ Kaf ל Lamed מ Mem נ Nun ס Samech ע Ayin פ Peh צ Tzadi ק Kuf ר Resh ת Tav

*The union of **Alpha** and **Omega**, in Greek, makes the verb αω, I breathe. And in Hebrew the union of the first and last letter in their alphabet, **Aleph** [bull's head] and **Tav** [the cross] makes ✝Ϸ in Ancient Hebrew or את in modern Hebrew - et, which the Rabbis interpret as the first matter out of which all things were formed, [see Gen 1:1]. The particle et, is untranslatable in English but, says Rabbi Aben Ezra, "it signifies the substance of the thing!" Jesus is the **Alpha** and **Omega**, or the **Aleph Tav**, in whom we live, and move, and have our being! He is indeed closer to us than the air we breathe! Don't waste a day waiting for another day!*

I have written the Ancient Hebrew alphabet below the modern square letter alphabet, corresponding each letter - its facinating pictograph meanings can be studied on this link,

https://www.studylight.org/lexicons/hebrew/ahl_alphabet.html

Introduction to Luke Chapter 3

Luke now brings John onto the stage. This final, and most significant of all the prophets, mirror-echoes Isaiah's voice, announcing God's highway into the wilderness. The Incarnate Word is coming to the rescue of humanity - every possible definition of distance and separation is addressed! And, all flesh shall see the salvation of our God! Mankind's authentic sonship is about to be redeemed!

[To appreciate the amazing context recorded here, please reference my introduction to chapter 4.]

Luke 3:21 Not only were all the people immersed into this prophetic, symbolic baptism, *[pointing to the death and resurrection event,]* but, to crown it all in the most significant and conclusive way, Jesus himself was baptized! *[Imagine the weight of this moment bearing upon Jesus! No wonder Luke records the fact that]* While Jesus was overwhelmed in prayer, the heavens opened! *(Luke again uses a most all inclusive word here, to emphasize the extent and significance of John's water baptism: ἅπας hapas, from ha, as a particle of union and pas, all; absolutely all or, every single one; [symbolically, Jesus' baptism includes the entire mass of humanity.])*

Luke 3:22 And here, in this open, heavenly dimension, the Holy Spirit alighted upon Jesus in a visible form - like a dove - and the Father's voice was clearly heard! My Son, you are my beloved one. In you rests my most glorious delight! *(The Triune, Father, Holy Spirit and Son, manifest in flesh! See Ps. 2:7 ... You are my son, today I have begotten you. Also Isa. 42:1 - in LXX ὁ παῖς μου my child, προσεδέξατο from προσ & δέχομαι - face to face embrace! You are my delight! τὸ πνεῦμά μου ἐπ᾽ αὐτόν my Spirit will continually rest upon him! [Note, my child! Not, servant as in the much later Masoretic text! See also Isa 52:13 and my comment in Rev 8:1])*

Now, Luke cleverly brings in the genealogy of the Incarnate word, immediately after Jesus' baptism. Leading us through the natural lineage of Jesus via the woman's seed. *["The seed of the woman shall crush the serpent's head!" Gen 3:15.]*

He brings in Joseph's Father-in-law, *[Eli was the father of Mary.]* Matthew writes the genealogy of Joseph, descended from David via Solomon, while Luke connects Jesus through Mary's lineage with David via Nathan! David named his son after the prophet Nathan who prophesied the Messianic kingdom over David's seed.

In order to highlight the significant meaning of the names that feature in the genealogy of Jesus, I have also employed the Ancient Hebrew alphabet, related to the Proto-Sinaitic alphabet. The earliest "Proto-Sinaitic" inscriptions are mostly dated to between the mid-19th (early date) and the mid-16th (late date) century BC. The discovery of the Wadi El-Hol inscriptions near the Nile River shows that the script originated in Egypt. These inscriptions strongly suggest a date of development of Proto-Sinaitic writing from the mid-19th to 18th centuries BC. https://en.wikipedia.org/wiki/Proto-Sinaitic_script

3:1 It was the fifteenth year of Tiberius, the Emperor. Pontius Pilate was governor of Judea, while Herod ruled Galilee. His brother Philip reigned in Iturea and Trachonitis and Lysanias was the ruler of Abilene. *(Herod the Great's kingdom was bequeathed to four heirs, of which Herod Antipas received both Perea and Galilee as a client state of the Roman Empire. Tetrarch, "ruler of a quarter".)*

3:2 It was at the time that Annas and Caiaphas were chief priests, that the word of God ¹ignited in John, the son of Zechariah, while he lived in the ²desert. *(The ρημα rhema of God ignited in him, ¹egeneto. ²Luke 1:80 And the child grew and became strong in spirit, and was in the wilderness till the day of his public appearance before Israel. [See Jn 1:19-36.])*

3:3 He emerged from the wilderness and travelled throughout the entire region of the Jordan, ¹publicly announcing a ²baptism of ³reformation; an ⁴engaging of a radical mindshift, celebrating mankind's redeemed ⁵identity and innocence! *(The first thing John does, is to publicly announce what his mission is all about. The word, κηρύσσω, ¹kerusso, to herald; to make an official announcement. The word ²baptizo from bapto, to immerse, to overwhelm. The Incarnate Word gives brand new meaning to the idea of baptism! This immersing into water symbolizes the remission of their sins pointing to mankind's true spirit fusion and inclusion in the Lamb of God who was about to rescue the world from their sins. John's baptism announces the incarnation; yet it communicates a mere prophetic picture of what Jesus' spirit baptism will fully interpret of humanity's co-inclusion and joint immersion into his death, resurrection and ascension. In the incarnation we have the prophetic word on exhibit, intercepting human history by assuming human form; thus we see divinity immersed into our humanity and declaring that there would be no stopping him from entering into our hell and deepest darkness. In dying our death, God would bring closure to every destructive mindset and futile fruit we inherited from Adam's fall. Just as he was raised out of the water in his baptism, we would be co-elevated together with him in his resurrection into newness of life! Hosea 6:2; Ephesians 2:5.*

The word, ³metanoia suggests a radical mindshift; a new awakening. The preposition ⁴eis, speaks of a point reached in conclusion. The words, αφεσιν αμαρτιων ⁵aphesin hamartioon, forgiveness of your sins, from apo, away from and eimi, I am! The word for sin, hamartioon - a distorted identity; from ha, negative and meros, form. Thus sin is that which separates one from one's true identity. The word, aphesis, occurs in Luke more frequently than in all the other N T writers combined.)

3:4 John here, most significantly mirrors the words of Isaiah; this is the moment! He lifted up his voice with great strength and cried out, [1]"Turn the wilderness into a highway! Make the ancient, [2]trodden out paths, [3]beautiful!" *(This is the unfolding of the prophetic moment which Isaiah saw 700 years ago! Isa 40:3-5. The word, ἑτοιμάζω [1]hetoimazō, meaning to prepare the way - from the oriental custom of sending persons before kings on their journeys, to level the roads and make them passable. Here in the Aorist Imperative case - ετοιμασατε etoimasate. According to the Greek scholar, Wallace, most Aorist Imperatives can be placed in one of two broad categories: the Ingressive, and Constative. The Constative stresses the urgency and the solemnity... "make this your top priority". The word, τρίβος [2]tribos, a track or rut that has been worn-out over time through much use. Thus, the maize of mankind's futile, criss-cross and cul-de-sac attempts to escape the clutches of the wilderness of their lostness in their trodden out paths of traditional beliefs and philosophies, are finally over! The word ευθύς [3]euthus, from eu, good; well done; beautiful and **tithemi**, to set in place. A voice cries: "In the wilderness prepare the way of the Lord, make straight in the desert a highway for our God. Every valley shall be lifted up, and every mountain and hill be made low; every crooked place shall be made straight, and the rough places smooth. And the glory of the Lord shall be revealed, and all flesh shall see it together, for the mouth of the Lord has spoken.)*

3:5 The Engineer of the universe will do this, with meticulous attention to detail! What seemed an impassible [2]chasm, will be seamlessly bridged! Every valley shall be filled up! Also, every mountain and hill be levelled out and every [1]crooked curve shall be straightened out! Even the rough places shall be made smooth! *(A seamless union is announced! The [1]question marks shall become exclamation marks! The word φάραγξ [2]pharagx is an abyss; a chasm; a rift or ravine hedged in by precipices. Every possible excuse mankind could ever have to feel separated from God is addressed! Every definition of distance is cancelled and every single obstacle and obstruction is about to be removed! The Judaean desert has many ravines, most of them deep, from 1,200 feet in the west to 600 feet in the east. It is an area with a special morphological structure along the east of the Judaean Mountains.)*

3:6 And this saving act of God shall be fully [1]realized by every individual. All flesh shall see and celebrate it together! *(The word, οψεται from [1]horao, to gaze upon; to see for oneself; to discern and perceive with the mind.*

"This phrase aptly describes Luke's Gospel which has in mind the message of Christ for all mankind. It is the universal Gospel." Says A.T. Robertson, [1863 – 1934] New Testament and Greek professor of the Southern Baptist Theological Seminary.)

3:7 John's [1]favorite message to the multitudes, coming out to be baptized by him, was, "[2]Offspring of vipers! Who showed you this [2]perfect escape route; away from the reach of her intended passion?" *("The [1]use of the following tenses is graphic. He continued to say, ελεγεν the Imperfect, and came forth, εκπορευομενοις the Present Participle; both these tenses denoting action in progress, or customary action; so that the sense is, he kept saying, or he used to say to those who were coming out, to the crowds of people which kept pouring out successively." Marvin Vincent.*

Brood of Vipers - [2]begotten of a mindset, poisoned by the serpent that snared mankind in the garden of Eden and abandoned them in the wilderness of a lost identity. See John 8:44 You are the offspring of a perverse mindset and you prove its diabolical parenthood in your willingness to execute its cravings. The intention was to murder humanity's awareness of their god-identity from the beginning since it is in violent opposition to the idea of the image and likeness of God in human form. It cannot abide the truth. Lying is the typical language of the distorted desire of the father of deception.

See John 1:51 & John 2:25. Just like Eve were deceived to believe a lie about herself, which is the fruit of the "I-am-not-tree". Also 2 Cor 11:3 I am concerned for you that you might pine away through the illusion of separation from Christ and that, just like Eve, you might become blurry-eyed and deceived into believing a lie about yourselves. The temptation was to exchange the truth about our completeness (I am), with the idea of incompleteness (I am not) and shame; thinking that perfection required your toil and all manner of wearisome labor!

*The verb, φυγειν from **pheogo**, escape, is an [2]Aorist Infinitive, which presents the action expressed by the verb as a completed unit with a beginning and end. The perfect way out. Beyond her [symbolic Eve] reach - ἀπὸ away from; τῆς her μελλούσης intended ὀργῆς passion - from **orgeomai**, to stretch one's self out in order to touch or to grasp something; to reach after or desire something.*

Like the prophet, Jonah, John sometimes seems to struggle with the idea of the free gift of forgiveness and righteousness. Jonah 3:10 & 4:1 Also later on in this chapter, Luke 3:19,20.)

3:8 [1]Now, [2]bear fruit that matches the [3]awakening of your authentic identity and your redeemed innocence! Quit seeking your origin in Abraham - your true lineage is found in God's faith; not in Abraham's efforts to bear children! See beyond mere flesh and discover God's power [4]raising the offspring of Abraham out of these stones! (*Again, the [1]Aorist Imperative is used; ποιησατε from [1]poieoo, "Get on with it!" Stressing the urgency and priority of the matter. [2]Let this [3]metanoia-moment conceive your offspring! Cease bearing the viper-fruit of a lost identity! [See notes on Luke 3:3]*

The word εγειραι [4]egeirai, from egeiroo, to arouse from sleep; to raise the dead! Here in the Aorist Infinitive which presents the action expressed by the verb as a completed unit with a beginning and end. In this parallel, Christ represents Sarah, the faith-mother who re-birthed you in the resurrection. The rock-hewn tomb represents Sarah's dead womb! 1 Pet 1:3. See Deut 32:18, "You were unmindful of the Rock that begot you, and you forgot the God who gave you birth.!"

"Simon, son of Jonah! I say, you are Mr. Rock! You're a chip of the old block!"

Isa 51:1 Hear me, pursuers of righteousness, seekers of Jaweh: Look to the rock from which you were hewn, and to the quarry from which you were dug. Isa 51:2 Look to your father Abraham, and to Sarah who bore you. For while he was still childless, I named him, Father of the multitudes of nations! And I blessed him and loved him [LXX] and multiplied him. Isa 51:3 For Jaweh comforts Zion. He comforts all her desolations, and he makes her wilderness like Eden, and her desert like the garden of Jaweh; joy and gladness shall be found in it, thanksgiving and the voice of singing and praise.

Our true I-am-ness is discovered in Jesus, not in Abraham! Before Abraham was, I am! πριν αβρααμ γενεσθαι εγω ειμι. John 8:58. See Luke 3:3 The words, αφεσιν αμαρτιων aphesin hamartioon, forgiveness of your sins, from apo, away from and eimi, I am! The word for sin, hamartioon - a distorted identity; from ha, negative and meros, form. Thus sin is that which separates one from one's true identity.

See Gal 3:6 Abraham had no other claim to righteousness but simply believing what God declared concerning him! Isaac confirmed God's faith, not Abraham's efforts. This is all we have in common with Abraham. [Righteousness reveals God's faith as responsible for mankind's salvation in direct contrast to their doing it themselves by keeping moral laws!] Gal 3:7 The conclusion is clear; faith and not flesh relates us to Abraham! [Grace rather than law is our true lineage. Ishmael represents so much more than the Muslim religion. Ishmael represents the clumsy effort of the flesh to compete with faith; the preaching of a mixed message of law and grace.] Gal 3:16 It is on record that the promise [of the blessing of righteousness by God's faith] was made to Abraham and to his seed, singular, [thus excluding his effort to produce Ishmael.] Isaac, the child of promise and not of the flesh mirrors the Messiah. Gal 3:27 To be immersed in Christ is to be fully clothed with him! He is your brand new wardrobe confirming your sonship! [From now on, the diaper days are over! "Our own righteousness, measured by our efforts to keep the law, compares to filthy rags!" Isa 64:6.] Gal 3:28 Nothing resembles your previous identity as Jew or Gentile, bond or free, male or female, Billabong or Gucci, now you are all defined in oneness with Christ! He is your significance and makes you beautiful! Gal 3:29 Since Christ is the seed of promise, it is only in our realizing our union with him [in the incarnation] that we are equally related to Abraham and heirs of the promise. Faith and not flesh, relates us to Abraham. [We inherit his righteousness by the same faith!])

3:9 [1]Most certainly will the very cause of the problem of a distorted identity be uprooted! Every tree that did not produce good fruit is about to be axed and thrown into the fire! The roots of those thought patterns that controlled your life, are powerfully addressed in this metanoia reformation. *(The word [1]ηδη - ede, from η, certainly, and δη de, without doubt. It is not merely getting rid of the cobwebs, but killing the spider! See my notes on "The other Tree" in 1 John 3:12. Also Isa 55:9-11. Its a waste of time to address behavior if the thought processes are wrong. See notes on the Lake of Fire at the end of Rev 19.)*

3:10 Then the throng of people desired to know how this radical mindshift would impact their practical lifestyle. *(The verb, ποιησωμεν poiesamen is in the Aorist Subjunctive Mood, which is similar to the Optative, expressing a wish. The Mood of the Greek verb expresses the mode in which the idea of the verb is employed. So, together with the preposition, **oun,** [therefore; consequently; in the light of,] the Aorist Subjunctive suggests, "Ok, we are ready to bear the fruit that matches our authentic identity and innocence [Luke 3:8] - what does it look like in our daily lives?)*

3:11 He said, "Those who have more clothes and food than others, should now see every opportunity to share what they have."

3:12 Also the tax people wanted to know how this would play out in their lifestyle.

3:13 John explained, "To now live from your redeemed identity and innocence, will radically impact the way you deal with money-matters! You no longer want to take any more money than the prescribed amount." *(The word πράσσω ¹prassō, speaks of one's general, habitual practice.)*

3:14 The soldiers also wanted to know about their lives and he said, "You would no longer want to intimidate anyone to make them tremble with fear when you show up! Neither would you threaten or blackmail people for favors. And you'll be totally content with your wages! Wow!"

3:15 The people were intrigued and wondered whether John perhaps, was the Messiah. *(See John 1:19-27.)*

3:16 John answered, "I symbolically immerse you in water but one, superior to me is about to come; he will immerse you in Spirit and in ¹fire! My baptism is preparing the way for him; I am not here to distract from him in any way, or to make a name for myself! I do not even qualify to be the slave that unties his sandals!" *(The Aramaic text reads "He will baptize you in the Holy Spirit and in light.")*

3:17 With his ¹winnowing shovel, he will thoroughly cleanse his threshing-floor with his own hands and gather the wheat into his granary. And he will burn the ²chaff with ³unquenchable fire. *(The word **ptuon**, is a winnowing shovel, as scattering like spittle; from **ptuō** to spit. The chaff represents those worthless philosophies and mindsets that have zero nutritional value. There will be no confusion between the chaff of religious traditions and the living incarnate word! The word, ἄχυρον **achuron** is a stalk of grain from which the kernels have been beaten out. Thus, Luke here also refers to the prophetic shadows as Paul does in Col 2:16,17 Do not let anyone therefore bring a restriction to your freedom by reviving religious rules and regulations pertaining to eating and drinking; all Jewish festivals, new moons, and Sabbaths have come to an end in Christ! [Their relevance only served to remind of the promise of Christ on an annual, monthly, and weekly basis. They carried the promise like a placenta would hold the unborn child, but became obsolete as soon as the child was born.] These things were only prophetic shadows; Christ is the substance.*

*The term ³**unquenchable** suggests that at no point in time will the fire of this spirit-dimension immersion, be ineffective. See notes on the Lake of Fire at the end of Rev 19.)*

3:18 And so, with many more words of encouragement John continued to proclaim these amazing good tidings of mankind's redeemed identity and innocence, to the crowds. *(The word parakaleo is so key to this sentence of Luke! Sadly, most translations read judgment and exhortation in this beautiful word! And yet they translate parakletos as the Comforter elsewhere! The word, parakaleo, alongside, closest possible proximity of nearness; and kaleo, to identify by name, to surname. Also, kinsman; intimate companion. See Rom 12:8. "...just be there alongside someone to remind them of their true identity." 1 Thessalonians 5:11 Continue, as you so eloquently do, to edify one another by cultivating the environment of your close association in your joint-genesis. [The word parakaleo is here translated as our joint-genesis.])*

3:19 Later on in his career, John *[sadly]* **also began to voice a strong political opinion by [1]speaking out against the Tetrarch, Herod for his many evils and also because he married his own sister-in-law, Herodias.** *(The word, elegcho means to refute, to point to the evidence as proof.*

This type of preaching out against sins, does not change anyone's life for real, plus it neutralizes the preacher's ministry! See my commentary note and rendering of 2 Tim 3:16, ...In many fragments of prophetic thought, God would heap up the evidence as proof [elegcho] of his purpose to raise fallen mankind up to be co-elevated with him, standing tall like a mountain-monument! The little stone that was cut out by no human hand is destined to strike that image of vanity and piety on its feet of iron and clay, to remove every trace of the substitute, man-made self-image with its glorious head of golden glitter and its silvery bust and bronze body. The stone will become in its place a Rock that fills the whole earth; the true image and likeness of God, restored and revealed in ordinary human life. [Dan 2:32-35.] "And the ends of the earth shall remember and return to the Lord!" [Psalm 22:27.])

3:20 This, was also the end of John's ministry and lead to his imprisonment and early death. *(I said, [sadly], since John's initial focus and voice pointed boldly to the Lamb of God, taking away the sins and distortions of the entire world! Having pointed him out, one would have imagined John to be one of the first disciples of Jesus, but later his disciples had more in common with the Pharisees than with Jesus! They would be fasting and praying with the Pharisees while Jesus' disciples were feasting and drinking with sinners and prostitutes!*

Many gifted people and their ministries have likewise "lost their heads" by becoming side-tracked into politics and philosophies.

I love Paul's uncluttered focus, 1 Cor 2:2 My mind is fully made up about you! The only possible way in which I can truly know you, is in the light of God's mystery, which is Christ in you! Jesus died mankind's death on the cross and thus brought final closure to any other basis of judgment! [Paul makes a very bold and radical statement, confining his ministry to "know" the full scope and consequence of the revelation of mankind's redeemed innocence as communicated in the cross of Jesus Christ! This is the essence of the mystery of God! "For I determined to know [- eido, to see, to perceive] nothing in you except Jesus Christ and him crucified." Nothing else! Not the latest gossip or popular news events! He says in 2 Cor 5:14, The love of Christ leads to this conclusion, one has died for all - therefore all died! From now on therefore, I no longer know ANYONE from a human point of view! Paul continues to unfold the mystery of our redeemed oneness! In the previous chapter, 1 Cor 1:30, he concludes that we are in Christ by God's doing; here he clearly points to Christ in us! [As Jesus declared in John 14:20.]])

3:21 Not only were [1]**all the people immersed into this prophetic, symbolic baptism,** *[pointing to the death and resurrection event,]* **but, to crown it all in the most significant and conclusive way, Jesus himself was baptized!** *[Imagine the weight of this moment bearing upon Jesus! No wonder Luke records the fact that]* **While Jesus was overwhelmed in prayer, the heavens opened!** *(Luke again uses* [1]*a most all inclusive word here, to emphasize the extent and significance of John's water baptism: ἅπας hapas, from ha, as a particle of union and pas, all; absolutely all or, every single one; [symbolically, Jesus' baptism includes the entire mass of humanity.])*

3:22 And here, in this open, heavenly dimension, the Holy Spirit alighted upon Jesus in a visible form - like a dove - and the Father's voice was clearly heard! My Son, you are my beloved one. In you rests my most glorious delight! *(See Ps. 2:7 ... You are my son, today I have begotten you. Also Isa. 42:1 - in LXX ὁ παῖς μου my child, προσεδέξατο from προσ & δέχομαι - face to face embrace! You are my delight! τὸ πνεῦμά μου ἐπ' αὐτόν my Spirit will continually rest upon him! [Note, my child! Not, servant as in the much later Masoretic text! See also Isa 52:13 and my comment in Rev 8:1])*

3:23 Jesus was approaching [1]**his 30th birthday when he began his ministry. It was the general opinion, that he was the son of Joseph. Jesus' grandfather, from his mother's side, was Eli, Joseph's father in law.** *(This was the* [1]*age when the priests and Levites began their service in the temple. Num 4:3. Yoseph יוסף - meaning, Jaweh* *has added.* Eli עלי - *elevation; to raise above; ascension. Luke here brings in Joseph's Father-in-law, for Eli was the father of Mary. "The seed of the woman shall crush the serpent's head!" Gen 3:15. Matthew writes the genealogy of Joseph, descended from David via Solomon, while Luke connects Jesus with David via Nathan! See, 2 Sam 5:14, David's children, born in Jerusalem: Shammua, Shobab, Nathan, Solomon.)*

3:24 Eli was the son of Matthat, the son of Levi, the son of Melchi, the son of Janna, who was the son of Joseph, *(Mattithiah,* מתתיה - *gift of Jaweh. Levi* לוי *joined in harmony. **Melki** מלך *my king.* **Janna** ינה - *Jaweh's seed - flourishing - in the Ancient Hebrew alphabet, the word **nah**,* נה *is the word,* 🜚 *which pictures a seed representing continuance. The man with the raised hands pictures a sigh of wonder; someone seeing something spectacular! The letter, he* ה *"behold," as when looking at a great sight; thus, meaning, "breath" or "sigh," as one does when seeing something wonderful and pointing it out.)*

3:25 son of Mattathias, son of Amos, son of Nahum, son of Esli, son of Nogah, *(**Mattathias** מתתיה - *gift of Jaweh; son of Amos* אמוץ *strength, mentally alert, courageous, brave; son of **Nahum**,* נחום *comfort. From Noah,* נח - *rest. The name **Esli** is probably a Greek transliteration of the Hebrew name* אצלי *Ezli, which doesn't occur in the Old Testament as anyone's name. The preposition* אצל *'esel, expresses proximity and is commonly translated in the OT, with, or beside. It is comparable to a similar Arabic verb that means to join; thus, a joint or joining. The son of **Nogah**,* נגה *brightness; also in Ancient Hebrew,* 🜚 *illuminating, morning.)*

3:26 son of Maath, son of Mattathias, son of Shimi, son of Josech, son of Joda, *(**Maath** מעט *(ma'at), small, describing concepts like soon, or near. Mattithiah,* מתתיה - *gift of Jaweh. **Shimi** שמעי *renowned; Josech or **Joseph** יוסף *Jaweh has added. **Judah** ידה *throwing or raising the hand in praise, thanksgiving and celebration.)*

3:27 son of Jochanan, son of Rhesa, son of Zerubbabel, son of Shealtiel, son of Neri, *(**Jochanan**,* יוחנן *grace gift of God. **Rhesa**, the Aramaic word* רישא *rē'šā', meaning head or prince.* זרבבל *Zerubbabel, "sown in Babylon". His parents saw in his birth the resurrection principle! Jesus speaks about the single grain of wheat that falls into earth and dies, and brings forth much fruit! John 12:24. Zerubbabel led the Jews back from Babylon about 520 BC, governed Judah, and rebuilt the temple. Luke uses the LXX [Septuagint] text, which gives his father as* שאלתיאל *Shealtiel "I have asked God".)*

56

3:28 son of Melchi, son of Addi, son of Cosam, son of Elmadam, son of Er, (*Melchi,* מלכי *my king. Addi,* עדי *- an adornment for testifying to one's position or rank. Cosam,* קסם *king's lips as oracles. Elmadam,* אלמודד *- from* אל *el [Elohim] and* דמם *damam - where the root meaning is all about beginnings; also blood. The noun* אדם *Adam, product or likeness-made-from-soil. Alternatively, the link word can be seen as* מדד *madad means to measure; thus, measured in Elohim. Elmadam is the son of Er* ער *awake; watchful. In Ancient Hebrew,* 𐤀 ⊙ *the eye and the head; the eye of understanding.*)

3:29 son of Josi, son of Eliezer, son of Jorim, son of Matthat, son of Levi, (*Son of* יוסי *Josi, he will be sustained of Jaweh. Eliezer* אליעזר, *God is his help; Jorem,* יורים *whom Jaweh has exalted; Mattat,* מתת *gift of God; Levi,* לוי *joined in harmony.*)

3:30 son of Simeon, son of Judah, son of Joseph, son of Jonam, son of Eliakim, (*Simeon* שמעון *heard; Ben-Judah,* יהודה *son of celebration/praise. Joseph,* יוסף *Joseph, meaning, Jaweh has added; Jonam,* יונם *Jaweh is a gracious giver; Eliakim* אליקים *my God raises up, he res-urrects!*)

3:31 son of Melea, son of Menna, son of Mattatha, son of Nathan, son of David, (*Melea,* מלאה *something fulfilled, that is, abundance of produce: - first of ripe fruit, fulness; in Ancient Hebrew, the letters,* 𐤖𐤌 *picture a mass of water and a shepherd' staff. A continuation of segments, which fill the whole. Like in a chain of words blended togeth-er to form a complete sentence. The son of Menna* מנא *- in Ancient Hebrew* ⊙𐤋𐤌 *soothsaying; seeing a future in the seed! Watching over something of importance. Mattithiah,* מתתיה *- gift of Jaweh. He was the son of Nathan,* נתן *means giver of gifts. A son of David,* דוד *the beloved - by Bathsheba. See the prophecy of Prophet Nathan in second Samuel chapter 7, "The LORD declares to you that the LORD will make you a house. When your days are fulfilled and you lie down with your fathers, I will raise up your offspring after you, who shall come forth from your body, and I will establish his kingdom. He shall build a house for my name, and I will establish the throne of his king-dom for ever. I will be his father, and he shall be my son. Your throne shall be established for ever" No wonder David named one of his sons after the prophet - and the very one Luke connects Jesus with, via Mary's lineage, Nathan!*)

3:32 son of Jesse, son of Obed, son of Boaz, son of Salmon, son of Nachshon, (*Son of Jesse* ישי *Jaweh is my husband - from* יאיש

from יֵשׁ *yêsh/yaysh. From an unused root meaning to stand out, or exist; entity; used adverbially or as a copula for the substantive verb* היה *hâyâh H1961 to breathe; to be; to exist; from the core of the name of Jaweh,* יהוה *"existing". Thus, the root word for Jesse,* היה *hajah, in the Ancient Hebrew is,* 𐤉𐤄 *- the pictograph* 𐤄 *represents one who is looking at a great sight with his hands raised. In David's father, Jesse, it is the one looking at the other in mirror likeness! See Act 13:22, Rom 15:12.*

This also reminds of the ה *that God added to Abraham's name! The letter* 𐤄 ה *is also the number 5, which is the number for grace!* **Obed,** עבד *bond servant, or in Ancient Hebrew, [remember to read from right to left:* 𐤃𐤁𐤏 *to see in the tabernacle, a door, where the earth and the sun meet on the horizon; a   worshipper; the son of Ruth and* **Boaz,** בעז *fleetness; strength; of sharp mind; son of* **Salmon,** שלמון *garment; son of* נחשון *Nachshon; named after the bronze serpent Moses made, pointing to the Messiah Redeemer! See Num 21:9,* נחושת *nechôsheth, bronze, and* נחש, *nachash, serpent. In ancient Hebrew,* 𐤕𐤔𐤅𐤇𐤍 *The ancient pictograph* 𐤍 *for the letter* n, *is a picture of a seed sprout, representing the idea of continuing to a new generation. Since it also resembles a snake, in the word we're studying here, the snake mentality is kept outside the tent wall and crushed! "The noun* נחש *nachash is the Bible's most common word for snake and always represent some kind of mental process. The identical verb* נחש *nachash means to divine or soothsay." [Abarim Publications' Biblical Dictionary.] The letter* ח 𐤇 *for the letter ch, like in the sound, ch in the word, Bach - it is a picture of a tent wall. The meanings of this letter is outside, as the function of the wall is to protect the occupants from the elements; the wall in the middle of the tent divides the tent into the male and female sections. It is also the letter 8. The letter,* 𐤅 *is the tent peg. The letter* 𐤔 *pictures two front teeth. This letter has the meanings of teeth, sharp and press, from the function of the teeth when chewing. It also has the meaning of two, again, both or second. And the* **tau,** *to mark; the final letter in the Hebrew alphabet,* ת *or,* 𐤕 *the cross in Ancient Hebrew! The cross will bring final closure to the snake-mindset.)*

3:33 son of Amminadab, son of Aram, son of Hezron, son of Perez, son of Judah, (*Amminadab* עמינדב *my people, ami* עמי *and nadab* נדב, *a freewill offering. In Ancient Hebrew,* 𐤍𐤃𐤁 𐤌𐤏 *with the first two letters, A and m,* 𐤌𐤏 *a picture of the eye, and* 𐤌 *as a picture of water or the sea representing mass, also heavenly dimension; and* 𐤍𐤃𐤁 *Nadab,* 𐤍 *seed, and a door on the horizon,* 𐤃 *and a tent/*

*tabernacle*מ. *Thus, his father prophesied in this name; "I see a door on the horizon and the multitudes of my people greatly advantaged by a freewill offering!" The son of* **Aram**, ארם *in ancient Hebrew,* ᴀᴍᕼᐂ *elevated; on high; Hezron prophesied in giving his son this name! Meaning, a great man who connects with the heavenly dimension.* **Paddan-aram** *is an area in Mesopotamia where Abram [father above] was born].* **Aram** *is the son of* **Hezron**, חצרון - *to inclose; also means to nourish, surrounded by a wall; the noun* חציר **hasir**, *means grass; also means leek [a bigger version of grass] and* חצצרה **hasosra**) *means trumpet; When the trumpets are sounded as an alarm of invasion, the inhabitants of the surrounding fields and villages, or yards, go to the protection of the walled city. The name,* **Perez** פרץ *denotes a breaking out of some enclosure; spreading out. In Ancient Hebrew,* ᴏᴧᕼ⌐ *To be spread out wide or widespread. The letter* פ *pe* ⌐ *means mouth then,* ר *r* ᕼ *pictures a head and the letter* צ *tzade tz* ᴏᴧ *is a picture a trail, leading up to a destination or stronghold. This name suggests a conversation that breaks out of mental molds and bonsai mindsets! [Judah's son by his daughter-in law who pretended to be a prostitute, Tamar - Gen 38:27-29, When the time of her delivery came, there were twins in her womb. And when she was in labor, one put out a hand; and the midwife took and bound on his hand a scarlet thread, saying, "This came out first." But as he drew back his hand, behold, his brother came out; and she said, "What a breach you have made for yourself!" Therefore his name was called Perez.] The son of* **Judah**, יהודה *praise; from* **jadah**, ידה *which pictures a hand thrown out in praise, gratitude and celebration! Ancient Hebrew,* 𐤟 ᴛᴃᴗᴧ *a hand, extended towards the door, where the earth and the sun meet on the horizon; The man with the raised hands pictures a sigh of wonder. This symbol, developed into the letter, he* ה *"behold," as when looking at a great sight; thus, meaning, "breath" or "sigh," as one does when seeing something wonderful and pointing it out.)*

3:34 son of Jacob, son of Isaac, son of Abraham, son of Terah, son of Nahor, *(The name,* יעקב *Jacob means, the heel-holder. Hos 12:3 In the womb he took his brother by the heel, And by his strength he was a prince with God. Also, Gen 25:23 And the Lord said to her, "Two nations are in your womb, and the two peoples, born of you, shall be divided; the one shall be stronger than the other; the elder shall serve the younger."*

The two come out of the same mold; yet they represent two types of people: one who understands his true identity by faith [authentic value]

*and one who seeks to identify himself after the flesh [performance-based].
Again, the law of performance versus the law of faith is emphasized in
order to prepare the ground for the promise-principle. Mankind's
salvation would be by promise and not by performance; i.e. it would
not be a reward for good behavior. No one will be justified by the tree of
the knowledge of good and evil; **poneros**, "evil," full of hardships,
annoyances and labor!) Son of **Isaac**, Jizghak* יצחק *laughter; son of*
Abraham אברהם; *the first two letters Aleph and Bet* אב *and in
Ancient Hebrew,* ע/פ *the head of a young bull - strength and* פ
*tent, house; strength of the house; thus, meaning father or head of the
house. Note that most of Abram's ancestors were already fathers at the
ages of 30 or 35; yet* **Terah** תרח *[meaning, delay] was 70 years old
before he had* **Abram**; אברם *his name suggests that Terah acknowledged
that he could not claim parenthood of this son, he was 'fathered from
above'! [Gen 11:12-26] Now imagine how nervous Abram was when
eventually he was 75 and still without child! That was when God met
with him and added to his name the 'ה he' of* יהוה *Jaweh's own name,
Abraham* אברהם. *And, in Ancient Hebrew,* ᴍᴍ⌁פ◌ע *The letter* ה *h,
in ancient Hebrew is* ⌁ *man with the raised hands pictures a sigh of
wonder."behold," as when looking at a great sight; thus, meaning,
"breath" or "sigh," as one does when seeing something wonderful and
pointing it out. The* ה *[he] is also the number 5, which is the number
for grace! In Arabic the word* **raham** *means drizzling and lasting rain. The
innumerable drops of water in the rain are like the stars mentioned in
Gen 15:5 "Look toward heaven, and number the stars, if you are able to
number them - so shall your seed be!" Now, imagine those innumerable
stars raining down upon the earth and each one becomes a grain of
sand! Gen 22:17 "I will indeed bless you, and I will multiply your
descendants as the stars of heaven and as the sand which is on the
seashore." In Genesis 17:4-5 God announces him as the father of the
masses of nations* אב המון גוים, **ab hamon goyim**; *The word* המון,
hamon, *does not express simply a large number, but the rain-like
noise that emerges from a unified, seething throng of people! Abraham's
identity, his name, was the echo of God's faith and his bold confession in
the absence of Isaac. The name change, similar to that of Simon to Rock,
reminds mankind to realize their original identity as sons of God, hewn
out of the Rock [Deut 32:18, Isa 51:1,2].* **Nahor** נחור, *nose; inhaling
the breath of life; in Ancient Hebrew,* ◌⌂ᴉ *a picture of a seed sprout,
representing the idea of continuing into a new generation;* ⌂ *for the
letter* **ch**, *like in the sound, ch in the word, Bach - it is a picture of a tent
wall, to protect the occupants from the elements outside; the head of a*

man, ℜ *can also represent the mind; thus, to see an offspring, protected in the tent walls of a man's mind. [Nahor is the grandfather of Abraham! Nahor's name carries the prophetic word in-spite of the seeming "delay" of the birth of his son and grandson!]*)

3:35 son of Serug, son of Reu, son of Peleg, son of Eber, son of Shelah, *(***Serug** in Greek, Σαρούχ or in Hebrew, שרוג **Saruck,** means intertwined. See in Ancient Hebrew,* LYℜ⤙ *a weaving or wrapping; picturing an entwined mind; securing provision for his flock. The letter,* שׂ *or* ס *"s", means thorn,* ⤙ *- this letter also has the meaning of a shield as thorn bushes were used by the shepherd to build a wall or shield to enclose his flock during the night to protect them from predators. The man's head for the letter r* ℜ*, means Rosh, or head; leader, also mindset; like the first word in Gen 1:1* בראשית *bereshet, from berosh, literally means "in the head" - creation is God's idea. Then the letter waw,* ו *or in Ancient Hebrew,* Y *represents a peg or hook, which are used for securing something; then the letter Gamma,* ג *or,* ⌐ *in Ancient Hebrew, is picture of a foot; meaning to walk and carry or gather food [to be stored in a protected area]. The son of* **Reu,** רעו *friend, Ancient Hebrew* Yℜ⌾ *to pasture, feed, shepherd. The son of* **Pelech** פלג *family-clan; Ancient Hebrew* ⤴⌐Yᴜ⌾ *the letter,* פ *pe* ⌾ *mouth, conversation; and l,* ל *shepherd's staff* ᴜ *then, the letter* ג *gamma, is the letter* ⌐ *foot; to walk, carry or gather.* **Eber,** עבר *the region beyond; and in Ancient Hebrew,* ℜⵔ⌾ *The son of* **Selach,** שלח*, sprout;* ⊞ᴜ⊔ *The shoots of a plant as sent out.*)

3:36 son of Cainan, son of Arphaxad, son of Shem, son of Noah, son of Lamech, *(***Cainan** קינן *and in Ancient Hebrew,* ⵔⵔ⤙⦿ *with a picture of the sun at the horizon and the gathering [*⤙ *outstretched hand] of the light, the* ⵔ *is a picture of continuance in the seed. The building of the nest and family; the foundation of community. In the ancestry of David, Luke agrees completely with the Old Testament.* **Cainan** *is included between* **Shelah** *and* **Arphaxad***, following the Septuagint text [though not included in the 1000 year later, Masoretic text followed by most modern Bibles]. See, https://journals.sagepub.com/doi/10.1177/0951820709103182 by Helen Jacobus. "This study suggests that Cainan (LXX Gen. 10.24; Gen. 11.12; [LXX A] 1 Chron 1:18; Jub 8:1-5; Lk 3:36-37), the missing thirteenth patriarch from Adam in the genealogical table in Masoretic text (MT) was known to the authors of the proto-MT, and the proto-SP. Using textual and chrono-genealogical analysis, it offers evidence to show that the thirteenth generation from the 13th generation from Adam had to contend with a curse."] It is amazing that Cain is included in the gene-*

alogy of Jesus and that every definition of curse is cancelled in the cross. Gal 3:13. Son of **Arphaxad** ארפבשד the name **Arphaxad** is difficult to interpret. Abarim publications suggests that since both ארף (a-r-p) and בשד (k-sh-d) do not exist in Hebrew, we should look for a possible combination of smaller words: ארי ('ari), lion; the פ may be a contraction of פה (peh), mouth; כ (ke) means as if and שד (shad) means breast. Possible meaning, 'like a lion suckling'. Son of שם **Shem**; meaning, name or renown. In ancient Hebrew, ᴧᴧᴗᴗ breath; it's plural form is שמים - *shemayim*, the heavens. Son of **Noach** נֹּחַ rest. Noach נֹּחַ found favor חֵן in the eyes of the Lord! See Gen 6:8, the same letters in reverse, as in a mirror reflection, חֵן **chen**, means, grace/favor. The son of למך **Lamech**; למך Lamech lived a total of 777 years; Arabic, meaning, strong and robust young man. In Ancient Hebrew, ᴗᴧᴧᴗ The shepherd staff leading towards the heavenly dimension. The shepherd staff represents the idea of "toward", as the staff is used to move a sheep toward a direction.)

3:37 son of Methuselach, son of Enoch, son of Jared, son of Mahalaleel, son of Cainan, (Son of מתושלח **Methuselach**, whose father, Enoch, walked with God, and didn't die! Metusalech was the oldest man in the Bible; he lived 969 years, and died the year of the flood. His name is most significant; from **met** מת man; also מת, **mot**, death. In Ancient Hebrew †ᴧᴧ and, **selach** שלח to sprout; the shoots of a plant as sent out. This is resurrection language! An unknown duration of time; sending, thus, a man on an apostolic mission. Son of Enoch [pronounce, **Chenok**], who lived 365 years and departed without dying; חנך **Chanuk**, ᴗᴗᴛᴛ meaning to inaugurate, train or dedicate. See John 10:22, Now in Jerusalem they were celebrating the feast of the renewal of the temple - which was in winter. [The Feast of Renewal, or new beginnings - ἐγκαίνια - egkainia, [1]en + kainos - also known as the Feast of Dedication or the Feast of Lights - which was three months after the Feast of Tabernacles - celebrated today as, חנוכה Hanukkah ᴛᴛᴗᴗᴗ❋ - the letter, ᴛᴛ for the letter ch, like in the sound, ch in the word, Bach - it is a picture of a tent wall, to protect the occupants from the elements outside; the ᴗ is a picture of continuance in the seed; the letter ג gamma, Y represents a peg or hook, which are used for securing something; the letter ᴗ, or כ k-sound, pictures a open palm presenting a free-will offering; then the ה he-sound, ❋ a picture of a man with his arms raised in wonder, looking at a great sight. This word celebrates the re-dedication of the temple! Also means to teach/train with understanding. The Hanukkah-feast [also called the Feast of Lights] lasts eight days from the 25th day of Kislev [in December] and commemorating the *rededication of the temple in 165 BC. by the Maccabees. This happened on the day, 3 years after the destruction of the temple. The significant happenings of the festival were the illumination of houses and synagogues, and the singing of Ps 30:1-3 "A psalm by David sung at the dedication of the temple. I will honor you highly, O LORD, because you have pulled me out of the pit. Psa 30:3 O LORD, you brought me up from the grave. You called me back to life!" The prophetic restoration of the temple in the resurrection!*

Jesus lived and communicated from his awareness of the prophetic significance of his life's mission in laying down his life and in co-raising fallen mankind together with him in his resurrection on the third day - Hosea 6:2, After two days he will revive us; on the third day he will raise us up! Ephesians 2:5. See John 2:19 To which Jesus responded, "The temple will be completely demolished by you and in three days I will raise it up!" The connection with the man Enoch is significant he was 365 years old when he - the temple of human life is resurrected and is rediscovered as God's address.]

Enoch *was the son of* ירד **Jared,** *in Ancient Hebrew,* ⊓ᕠᗐ *laying a mental hold on the door on the horizon. He was the son of* מהללאל **Mahalaleel,** מהלל *(mahalel), Proverbs 27:21 man is a container of praise; from* הלל *(halal) means to shine [like the stars]; to cheer with great excitement; letting it rip; to be raving mad. The Ancient Hebrew word is* ᒉᒉ⊕ *with,* ⊕ *a picture of a man with his arms raised in wonder, looking at a great sight. The* ᒉ *is a shepherd staff representing the idea of "toward", as the staff is used to move a sheep toward a direction. Combined these letters mean "a looking toward something" such as the looking toward a light in the distance. The stars have always been used to guide the traveler or shepherd to find his home or destination. The double* ᒉᒉ *reinforces the certainty in the prophetic idea.*

Son of **Cainan** קינן *in Ancient Hebrew,* ᔑᔑᗐ⊙ *with a picture of the sun at the horizon and the gathering [ᗐ outstretched hand] of the light, the* ᔑ *is a picture of continuance in the seed. The building of the nest and family; the foundation of community.)*

3:38 son of Enos, son of Seth, son of Adam, son of God. *(Son of* אנוש *Enos. The root* אנש **anish** *isn't used as verb in the Bible, but in Arabic, a sister language,* **Yanish** *means: gift of God. In Ancient Hebrew* ᒐᎩᔑᕒ *the strength* ᕒ *of the seed* ᔑ *shall prevail* Ꭹ *[a tent-peg securing the tent] and crush* ᒐ *the serpents head! See Gen 3:15 your seed shall crush* ⊂ᒐ *the serpents head -* שׁוּף *crush and in Ancient Hebrew,* ⊂ᒐ *"sharp teeth in the mouth"; also to strike like a serpent.*

The letter symbol, ⊔⊔ *pictures the two front teeth; meaning, sharp and press, from the function of the teeth when chewing.*

Son of Set, שת *resurrection of that which was lost in death. Seth was the third son of Adam and Eve. Eve considered him to be a resurrection of her dead son, Abel. "And Adam knew his wife and she bore a son and called his name Seth. For God has ¹resurrected anther seed for me, instead of Abel, whom Cain slew." The text reads,* שת כי שת *Gen 4:25. She called his name* שת *Set, because God* שת *[resurrected] another seed for me! Now, just from reading this Hebrew text of Gen 4:25, I took the liberty to translate Set to mean resurrection, before I even looked at the LXX Greek text where the word* εξανεστησεν, *¹eksanastesen, is used! The word* **eksanastsis** *is from the preposition* **ek**, *out of, pointing to the source and* **anastasis**, *resurrection! God has resurrected a seed for me! See my notes on Zerubbabel in verse 27. Also,* **1 Peter 1:3** Εὐλογητὸς ὁ Θεὸς καὶ πατὴρ τοῦ Κυρίου ἡμῶν Ἰησοῦ Χριστοῦ, ὁ κατὰ τὸ πολὺ αὐτοῦ ἔλεος ἀναγεννήσας ἡμᾶς εἰς ἐλπίδα ζῶσαν δι'ἀναστάσεως Ἰησοῦ Χριστοῦ ἐκ νεκρῶν. *See this in Mirror Bible. With reference to Cain killing Abel, please also see 1 John 3:8-12 in the Mirror Bible. We have the prophetic picture of a scapegoat repeated here in Genesis 4. Not only in the sacrifice that Abel brought; but also in him being murdered by his brother! Just like we would one day murder our brother Jesus!*

Son of Adam, אדם - *product or likeness-made-from-soil;* אֲדָמָה *adamah, earth. Image and likeness "earthed" in Adam; in flesh! Son of God. El,* אל *with reference to the plural form, Elohim -* אלהים *Father, Son and Spirit; as in Genesis chapter 1.)*

64

Introduction to Luke Chapter 4
Facing the wilderness of a lost identity.

The echo of Isaiah's voice in John's mouth, still hangs strong in the atmosphere! "A voice cries: In the wilderness prepare the way of the Lord, make straight in the desert a highway for our God. **Every** valley shall be lifted up, and **every** mountain and hill be made low; **every** crooked place shall be made straight, and **all** the rough places smooth. And the glory of the Lord shall be revealed, and all flesh shall see it together, for the mouth of the Lord has spoken." *(Isa 40:3-5)*

With the last of the prophets, John the Baptist, who recently emerged from the wilderness in a dynamic and vibrant prophetic voice, the attention now shifts to Jesus. The event of Jesus' own, dramatic baptism, endorsed the awesomeness of his mission!

He now stands on the threshold of the Jordan, in the full awareness of its profound, prophetic setting and significance. He reflects on his massive assignment, as Savior of the world, he would be the mirror-doorway for mankind, out of the same wilderness where Israel was snared, in a forgotten identity, having been persuaded by their leaders that they are mere grasshoppers compared to the giants of their imagination - they "appeared" to be like grasshoppers compared to the enemy, they would still have to conquer. An entire, already "redeemed from slavery-generation", dies on the wrong side of the promise by believing a lie about themselves! This clearly pictures those mindsets and lies that we have been taught, that dwarfs us into insignificance and keeps us from possessing the promised land of our authentic lives, revealed and redeemed in Jesus. The enemy is not "the devil" - it's the un-renewed mind. Finally, their children are led prophetically by Joshua into the promised land of their forgotten identity, after 40 wasted years! *([Joshua 4:19] And the people came up out of Jordan on the tenth day of the first month. [1406 B.C.] Notice the exactness of the narrative. The first month is elsewhere called Abib; the time of the Passover, or Pasach, פסח protecting and rescuing. From an Arabic root which means to expand; to save. In Ancient Hebrew it is, חש×☉ [reading from right to left, the letter פ pe ☉ means mouth; then the letter, שׂ or ס "s", which means thorn, ☆ - this letter also has the meaning of a shield as thorn bushes were used by the shepherd to build a wall or shield to enclose his flock during the night to protect them from predators. Then, the letter, חש for the letter ch, like in the sound, ch in the word, Bach - it is a picture of a tent wall, to protect the occupants from the elements outside. Thus, the mouth speaking the prophetic word, announcing the good news of salvation from every possible threat.)*

A new era awaits. Here, where the new generation of Israel was led through the Jordan by Joshua into the promised land. Their leader, Moses [*"the law-man"*] died and by then, also the entire old generation in their blindfold-mode of unbelief. See the book of Numbers 13:33 *(Original name of the book of Numbers,* במדבר *Bemidbar, in the wilderness.)* Also Josh 2:11.

The site where Jesus was baptised is called Bethany in John 1.28. The "Place of Crossing". After the crossing, Joshua commanded to take out 12 stones and place them in the next camping place, Gilgal: "these stones shall be for a memorial unto the children of Israel for ever." [Joshua 4.7] Here, they also kept their first Pascha in the land of Canaan. With the significant root meaning hidden in the word, פסח Pasach - to save; to expand, they were certainly celebrating the joy of salvation from slavery and the detour of a lost and forgotten identity! As John was baptising here, he probably referred to these 12 stones when he said: "God is able to raise up children unto Abraham out of these stones." [Matthew 3.9.] A new generation is prophesied by John - the resurrection generation, emerging out of the rock-hewn tomb together with the risen Jesus! Eph 2:5; 1 Pet1:3.

Jesus' baptism would be the launch of his three year ministry. Overwhelmed by the enormous magnitude of this moment and his mission as Savior of the world, most spectacularly endorsed by the Father and Holy Spirit, he knew, that in the genius of God, he would fulfil prophetic scripture and crush the "serpent's head". He would bring closure to the haunting dilemma of a forgotten identity; the "I am not-mindset" that Adam and Eve plunged their offspring into; repeated again in Israel's account of their forty year wilderness-detour that kept them out of their "promised land". Picturing the prophetic re-possessing of the nations of the world, fully embraced under the Lordship of their Maker and true husband. The promised land is not a mere geographic spot on the planet, but indeed, all of human life, both individually and collectively made whole and living in a healed world! Your person, body soul and spirit - all that you are in your amazing uniqueness, is your personal "Promised Land!"

He would die humanity's death as his doorway into their darkness of a lost identity and gloriously co-quicken and co-raise them again into the fullness and newness of their redeemed, authentic life.

Fully infused and prompted by Holy Spirit, Jesus intentionally turns back, away from the river Jordan into the wilderness where he embarks on a forty day fast in order to victoriously face the same diabolic scrutiny that snared humanity in Adam and Eve, and dramatically displayed in Israel's detour in the wilderness of their unbelief. Jesus countered these, with the words of Deuteronomy which Moses wrote while Israel was encamped "beyond the Jordan" [Deut. 31.9] See Luke 4:1-13.

See my commentary note on Luke 3:7 "Brood of Vipers" - begotten of a mindset, poisoned by the serpent that snared mankind in the garden of Eden and abandoned them in the wilderness of a lost identity. Also, John 8:44 You are the offspring of a perverse mindset and you prove its diabolical parenthood in your willingness to execute its cravings. The intention was to murder humanity's awareness of their god-identity from the beginning since it is in violent opposition to the idea of the image and likeness of God in human form. It cannot abide the truth. Lying is the typical language of the distorted desire of the father of deception.

Note, John 1:51 & John 2:25. Just like Eve were deceived to believe a lie about herself, which is the fruit of the "I-am-not-tree". And, 2 Cor 11:3 I am concerned for you that you might pine away through the illusion of separation from Christ and that, just like Eve, you might become blurry-eyed and deceived into believing a lie about yourselves. The temptation was to exchange the truth about our completeness *(I am)*, with the idea of incompleteness *(I am not)* and shame; thinking that perfection required your toil and all manner of wearisome labor!

Moses fasted for forty days here; both times he went up the mountain of Horeb [Sinai] to receive an external make-shift law; as an interim arrangement, which in time would prove Israel's failure to engage their godlikeness in their lifestyle through their efforts and performance. The law also prophetically pointed to the fact that their only true redemption would be by the Messiah who would die humanity's death and bring closure to a redundant system and then, in his resurrection, he would gloriously reboot the default settings of the agape-law written in human hearts by design. [Deut 9 and 10.]

Also Elijah, in a miserable mood, feeling frustrated and a failure in his ministry and fleeing from Jezebel, just like Israel receiving manna from above, he, on the offset of his long journey and 40 day fast, is strengthened and sustained supernaturally by food he did not labor for. See 1 Kings 19:11 Then the Lord said to Elijah, "Go, stand in front of me on the mountain. I, the Lord, will pass by you." Then a very strong wind blew. The wind caused the mountains to break apart. It broke large rocks in front of the Lord. [*Symbolic of the tablets of stone!*] The Lord was not in the wind. After that wind, there was an earthquake. The Lord was not in the earthquake. 1 Kings 19:12 After the earthquake, there was a fire. The Lord was not in the fire. [*Elijah here encounters a replay of Moses' encounter in receiving the law*] After the fire, there was a quiet, gentle voice. And the Lord spoke to him...

Consider the contrast between the dramatic experience Moses had and then the ***whispering***, הממד *demamah small* דק *dak* voice that spoke to Elijah; showing the difference between the two dispensations of law and grace.

This is how Elijah experienced the sound of God's voice: The word דממה *demamah*, whispering; and in Ancient Hebrew, 𐤄ᛗ⊔ a door on the horizon into the heavens with the letter ה *he*, in ancient Hebrew, 𐤔 a man with the raised hands pictures a sigh of wonder; "behold," as when looking at a great sight; thus, meaning, "breath" or "sigh," as one does when seeing something wonderful and pointing it out. The ה *[he]* is also the number 5, which is the number for grace! Here, the word, דממה suggests the awe of likeness recognized! See Strongs number H1827 and H1819, דמה likeness; also in Ancient Hebrew, 𐤔ᛗ⊔ likeness; one who resembles his father!

Then the word translated, small, דק *dak*, is used; meaning to be broken into small, bite-size pieces; crushed [*like grain*]. In Ancient Hebrew, ⊔ᛝ again, a picture of a door, meaning access into a new space, also the palm of the hand offering a gift [*crushed grain*] from heaven. Also, incense beaten small as in Lev 16:12 "And he shall take a censer full of coals of fire from the altar before the LORD, and two handfuls of sweet incense beaten small; and he shall bring it within the veil."

See Hebrews 12:18-29. Here is verse 18 We are not talking of a visible and tangible mountain here, one spectacularly ablaze in a setting of dark blackness and tempestuous winds. *(Witness the vivid contrast between the giving of the law and the unfolding of grace; the exclusiveness of the one and the all inclusive embrace of the other. The dramatic encounter of Moses on the mountain is by far exceeded by the mountaintop experience to which we are now welcomed and elevated to, in Christ! Mankind is fully represented and co-seated together with Christ in heavenly places! Eph 2:5, 6, Hosea 6:2.)*

Also Matthew's account in chapter 17 of the mount of transfiguration, with both Moses and Elijah present, representing the law and the prophets, both now concluded in the mission of Jesus.

See Gal 3:19 So what is the use of the law then? The law was doing you a [1]favor, in that it was [2]positioned as a [3]mirror-measuring rod as an intermediary arrangement to make people aware of the extent of their out of sync-ness with the life of their design and at the same time point them to the promise of a Redeemer, the Messianic seed! It was given by celestial messengers to Moses. *(Paul uses the word [1]charin here - God graced us with the law as a mirror-reminder of our original identity! The word, [2]prostithemi means to be positioned in the face of; like a mirror. The word [3]parabasis suggests a standard/measuring stick; from para, close proximity and basis, footprint; thus compared to the standard rule, mankind's out of sync-ness with their default settings became obvious.]* Gal 3:20 With Abraham there was no middleman; it was just God! Gal 4:4, The Son arrived, commissioned by the Father; his legal passport to the planet was his mother's womb. In a human body exactly like ours he lived his life subject to the same scrutiny of the law. Gal 4:5 His mandate was to rescue the human race from the regime of the law of performance and announce the revelation of their true sonship in God. Also Rom 3:21 We are now talking a completely different language: the gospel unveils what God did right not what we did wrong! Both the law and all the prophetic writings pointed to this moment! God's dealing with mankind is based on the fact that their conscience continues to bear witness to their original design. Romans 7:22.

Jesus is the end of the Law! Rom 10:4. What does that mean? Does grace now lower the standard of "the requirements" of the law!? No grace replaces our willpower as the operating system of our lives and introduces us to the operating system of Agape, personified in the man Jesus Christ as in a mirror! Our authentic life - the life of our design is redeemed! This is the law of faith or as Paul also calls it, the law of the spirit, of life in Christ Jesus! Rom 3:27, Rom 8:2.

Now, even looking at the ten commandments as in a mirror rather than as in a duty- or guiltdriven display window of requirements, changes everything!

[handwritten annotation: I am take 2... goes back to redeem, undo, past]

4:1 And Jesus, fully infused and ¹prompted by Holy Spirit, ²intentionally turns back, away from the river Jordan into the wilderness and embarks on a forty day fast in order to victoriously face the same diabolic scrutiny that snared humanity in Adam and Eve, and later dramatically displayed in Israel's detour in the wilderness of their unbelief. *(See the book of Numbers 13:33 [Original name of the book, רבדמב Bemidbar, in the wilderness.] They have completely forgotten their god-identity. Also Josh 2:11.*

The verb ¹egeto, ἤγετο [Imperfect Passive - pointing to an uninterrupted state of companionship] from agoo, to lead; to accompany. The word, ²υπεστρεψεν from hupo, under and strepho, to turn; to turn back; to return. In the symbolic significance of his baptism, reflecting his death, he now goes into our hellish wilderness in order to disengage every demonic onslaught on our identity and sonship. He is in a Holy Spirit-encounter in the wilderness, ἐν τῷ Πνεύματι ἐν τῇ ερημω; in the very wilderness where an already redeemed from slavery Israel, was snared into believing a lie about themselves - "we are not image bearers of God - we are reduced to grasshopper-status, compared to the giants!" Also, the very wilderness Adam and Eve landed up in, outside of the garden of abundance -Eden; because of the same temptation, "you are not the image and likeness bearer of Elohim.")

4:2 When the forty days were concluded, he felt famished, having not taken anything to eat at all. *(An "opportune time" [See verse 13] presents itself; see John 4:6-9 Since it was already midday and Jesus felt exhausted and thirsty from their day and a half walk, [40 miles from Aenon] he decided to wait at the well while his disciples would go into the village to buy food. [Having left the Place of Springs, Aenon early the previous morning, one can just imagine how Jesus' mind drifted to the fountain theme! The life Jesus lived in a human body was no different to ours; he felt the same weariness, hunger and thirst we would, yet he never forgot what manner of man he was. He lived convinced and conscious of who he was. This was his secret; this was how he overcame every temptation victoriously.] John 4:7 When a local Samaritan woman finally arrived to draw water, Jesus immediately asked her for a drink. Jn 4:9 The woman obviously anticipated this request and was ready with her response, "You are a Jew, aren't you? So why would you expect to get anything for free from a Samaritan woman?" Within the politics of the day, Jews looked down upon the Samaritans and had no dealings with them. [She knew very well how strategically en-route this precious well was and what political leverage it gave her over weary Jewish travellers!]*

*Temptation is often about looking at scripture in a different light..."It is written..." vs. "it is **also** written..." Or, "You have heard it said," then Jesus continues with, "But I say unto you!")*

4:3 The Devil had an immediate suggestion, "If you really are the son of God, then prove it and do your magic! Tell this stone to become a loaf of bread!" *(Not long after this, he would turn water into wine to satisfy other people's thirst!)*

4:4 And Jesus answered, "It is written that man shall not live on bread alone." *(See John 6:30 So Jesus, if it is your job to get us to believe, we need to see more signs! John 6:31 How do you compete with Moses? Our fathers ate the manna in the wilderness - as it is written - He gave them bread from heaven to eat. [The rabbis quoted Psalm 72:16 to prove that the Messiah, when he comes, will outdo Moses with manna from heaven. Ps 72:16 "There shall be a handful of corn in the earth upon the top of the mountains; the fruit thereof shall shake like the cedars of Lebanon: and they of the city shall flourish like grass of the earth. KJV [A handful of corn - five loaves here [in John 6] and in the following year's Passover Jesus' own body would be the bread broken on the mount of Golgotha!]*

Deuteronomy 8:3 And he [1]treated you gently in the wilderness of your unbelief and fed your hunger there with manna, which you did not know, nor did your fathers know; that he might show you that there is a bread that comes from above, that you did not labor for! Your labor and achievement can never satisfy your deepest longings. The life of our design hungers to be completely sustained by [2]that Word which proceeds out of the mouth of the LORD. [Some translations say, "[1]humbled you" but in 2 Samuel 22:36 the word [1]עַנְוָה Anahvah is translated, "Your [1]gentleness made me great." We are designed to live by [2]every Word which proceeds out of the mouth of the LORD. The Hebrew word כל Kohl from בלל Kalal, often translated, "every" actually means complete; thus, the word in its most complete context. The destiny of the word was so much more than a scroll or page in a book, it always was the Incarnation - Jesus, the Word made flesh!] He freed us from our slavery and led us gently like a shepherd through the wilderness of our own unbelief and made known to us that our authentic hunger is not for the bread we labor for, but, just like the prophetic picture of manna from above, we can only be truly satisfied by the Word from above; that Word which mirrors our redeemed joint-genesis and eternal oneness!]

John 6:32 Jesus reminded them that it wasn't Moses who gave them the bread from heaven - My Father is the one who gives the real bread from heaven! [The manna was a prophetic pointer to the Messiah!]

John 6:33 For the bread from God that comes down from heaven is that which gives life to the entire world! [Mankind is designed, not to define life by the bread-harvest of their own labor, but by daily feasting on every Word that proceeds from God's mouth, mirrored in its most complete language, the Incarnation. Again the Hebrew word בל **Kohl** *from* בלל **Kalal**, *often translated, "every" actually means complete; thus, the word in its most complete context. The Word that is face to face before God from before time was, is now made flesh, radiating the invisible Father's character and image in human form, as in a mirror! The incarnation is the global language of the Planet! Paul says in 2 Cor 3:2,3, The living Epistle is known and read by all in their mother-tongue language.])*

4:5 He then showed him all the kingdom's of the inhabited world in a split second.

4:6 And said to him, I will give you the glory and control of all these kingdoms since it was handed over to me and I can do with it whatever I please!

4:7 It's all yours if you worship me. *(First temptation was to question his sonship; then he offers him something he already has. Ps 24:1 - like a thief trying to sell stolen property which was never his to begin with.)*

4:8 Jesus responded with, "Get out of my face Satan! Scripture says, you shall worship the Lord your God with undivided [1]**adoration."** *(If love is very intense you would say "latreuō" - λατρεύω to [1]adore.)*

4:9 Then he led him to Jerusalem and brought him to the wing of the temple and challenged him to cast himself down, if he really is the son of God. *(The word here is πτερύγιον [1]pterugion, wing, from the Latin pinnaculum, a diminutive of pinna [wing]. It may refer to Herod's royal portico which overhung the Kedron Valley and looked down some four hundred and fifty feet. Josephus, Ant. XV. xi. 5. This was on the south of the temple court. Hegesippus says that James the Lord's brother was later placed on the wing of the temple and thrown down.)*

4:10 It is written, he says, that God would command his celestial shepherd-messengers to protect you from any harm.

4:11 They would bear you up on their hands and protect you so that you will not even stumble over a stone. *(Ps 91:11,12.)*

4:12 Again, Jesus quoted Deuteronomy and said, you shall not put the Lord your God to the test. Testing is not trusting.

4:13 This concluded the devil's scrutiny and he departed until an opportune time. *(See Luke 4:2.)*

4:14 Then Jesus, empowered in spirit, turned to Galilee. His [1]fame spread throughout the entire region. *(The word, ευφημα [1]ephema, is where our English word, fame or famous derives from; see Phil 4:8.)*

4:15 He was [1]teaching regularly in their synagogues and was held in high esteem by everyone. *(The verb εδιδασκεν edidasken, is in the Imperfect Tense; thus, he was in the habit of teaching.)*

4:16 After some time, he also came to Nazareth where he was raised. It was his custom to go to the synagogue on the Sabbath.

4:17 The scroll of Isaiah the prophet, was handed to him and he stood up to read. *(The Syriac Sinaitic manuscript has it that Jesus stood up after the attendant handed him the scroll.)*

4:18 He opened the scroll and rolled it out in order to find the specific place where the following was written, "The Spirit of the Lord is upon me, because he has [1]anointed me to announce [2]glad tidings to a [3]starving people; he has [4]commissioned me to announce the freedom of [5]forgiveness *[their true I-am-ness]* to those [6]held captive at spear-point by their guilt and shame; also, the blind may now look up and be restored in their sight! I am anointed [7]to send out those who are bruised and traumatized, into the freedom of their redeemed [8]innocence. *(The verb, εχρισεν [1]echrisen from χρίω chrio, to smear with the hand; from xeir, hand; to anoint; see the Hebrew for Messiah, משיח to anoint; from mashach, משׁח to draw the hand over, to measure. [Analytical Hebrew and Chaldee Lexicon, B Davidson.] The anointing is the true measure of our lives, not our mental- or muscle-effort to produce results.*

Our use of the word, "christening" is really a word that means the endorsing of our in-Christness.

To announce good tidings, ευαγγελισασθαι [2]euangelisasthai, in the Aorist Infinitive tense, which presents the action expressed by the verb as a completed unit with a beginning and end. The Anointed Christ is the Good News in its most complete context.

The word, πτωχός [3]ptochos; to be in a starving and beggarly state.

The Perfect Active Indicative απεσταλκεν [4]***apestalken*** *denotes an action that has been completed in the past and the results of the action are continuing on in this moment, in full effect; of the word,* **apostellō**, *to commission. Then, the same word,* **apostello**, *but this time in the Aorist Infinitive, αποστειλαι* [8]***apostelai***, *which presents the action expressed by the verb as a completed unit with a beginning and end; thus, a sending out of the enclosure of their trauma and hurts, since the door that shut them in, no longer exists.*

The word, αἰχμαλωτός, [6]***aichmalotos***, *from* **aichme**, *spear and* **halosis**, *to capture, thus, to arrest at spear point.*

Then the opening of the blind eyes suggests, a complete change of perspective - a looking upward! The word, ἀναβλέπω **anablepō**, *from* **ana**, *upward and* **blepo**, *to see.*

The word translated forgiveness, or remission is the word ἄφεσις aphesis from [8]***aphieimi***; *from* **apo**, *away from, and* **hieimi** *an intensive form of* **eimi**, *I am; thus, forgiveness is in essence a restoring to your true 'I-am-ness.' The injury, insult, shame, hostility or guilt would no longer define the individual.)*

4:19 I announce that the Jubilee year of the Lord has come! This is the liberation celebration of the Lord, embracing humanity home! *(Lev. 25,10 "You will declare this fiftieth year sacred and proclaim the liberation [Greek aphesis] of all the inhabitants of the land. This is to be a jubilee for you". In the Greek translation of the Old Testament the relation between jubilee and liberation is even closer because the Hebrew term יובל jubel is not translated into Greek as it was in the Latin of the Vulgate (jubilaeus) and in other languages, it has been translated as "liberation [aphesis; see my commentary of this word in the previous verse]" (Lev 25,13), or "year of liberation" (Lev 25,10) or again "sign of liberation" (Lev 25,11-12) In Hebrew, יובל or in ancient Hebrew Ⴑ⅄ⰏⲨ⅃ to shepherd someone safely and securely home. See Lev 25:10 in the LXX "...and each of you shall return to his home!" Luke 15! The prodigal son came to himself when he returned home! Back to his true I-am-ness!)*

4:20 Jesus then rolled up the scroll and gave it back to the attendant and sat down, while everyone's eyes were fixed on him. *(They knew that the entire Messianic expectation hinges on this Scripture; the big question is, when?!)*

4:21 He then proceeded to say to them, "Everything contained in this scripture, its complete prophetic, Messianic and Jubilee

significance is now fulfilled - in your ears! You don't have to wait for another day or another time! Within your grasping and accurate hearing, today becomes your day! This is the fulness of time!"

4:22 For a moment, everyone was touched and filled with wonder at the words of grace that poured out of his mouth. Until they began to mutter amongst themselves and said, "Hey, but this is Joseph's son, no?" *(The use of* ouchi, *the intensive form of* ouk - *in a question, expects the affirmative answer. They began to voice the same question rising from the typical diabolos-mindset: Who is this guy!? How can a son of Joseph now suddenly emerge as the "Messiah? Knowing Jesus from a mere human point of view, veils him from you, and blocks the mirror impact for you to now also discover yourself! - see Math 16:13-19; 2 Cor 5:16.)*

4:23 And he said to them, "You will most certainly quote this proverb to me, "Doctor, prove your medicine skills by curing yourself!" And you will insist, "C'mon! We want to see signs as evidence! Do all the things here, that we've heard you do in Capernaum!" *(He is facing the same scrutiny he did in the wilderness.)*

4:24 This saying is equally relevant, "No prophet is recognized in his home town."

4:25 Surely there were many widows in Israel during Elijah's time; the famine was severe everywhere since it hasn't rained for three-and-a-half years.

4:26 Yet Elijah was not sent to any of them, but only to a widow at Sarepta in Sidon.

4:27 There were also many lepers in Israel in the prophet Elisha's time; yet only Naaman the Aramean was cleansed. *(Both the Aramaic and Greek texts have "Naaman the Aramean" or "descendant of Aram." The Arameans inhabited what is now Syria. 2 Kings 5:1-3 Naaman was general of the army under the king of Aram. It so happened that Aram, on one of its raiding expeditions against Israel, captured a young girl who became a maid to Naaman's wife. One day she said to her mistress, "Oh, if only my master could meet the prophet of Samaria, he would be healed of his skin disease.")*

4:28 On hearing this, everyone in the synagogue exploded with rage!

4:29 They jumped to their feet and threw Jesus out of town; then they escorted him up to the edge of the hill on which

Nazareth was built and tried to throw him over the cliff. *(Again, a replay of his temptation in the wilderness experience!)*

4:30 But he left them grabbing at thin air.

4:31 He then went to Capernaum, a town in Galilee where he frequently taught in their synagogues on the Sabbaths.

4:32 His teachings kept [1]breaking the mold that their minds were trapped in! The word he taught, [2]mirrored [3]in them, their true [4]I-am-ness. *(The word, εξεπλησσοντο is the Imperfect Passive Indicative - thus, it kept happening! From, ἐκπλήσσω [1]ekplesso, ek out of, and πλάσσω plassō to form; to mold; to shape or fabricate something from clay or wax. The word explessonto also means, to strike a person out of his senses by some strong feeling, such as wonder or joy" [Gould]. Then follows the sentence, [3]en exousia aen ho logos autou - ἐν ἐξουσίᾳ ἦν ὁ λόγος αὐτοῦ - [3]in the echo of I am, his word continues to be I am... The word, ην - aen, is the Imperfect Indicative of eimi, I am - thus, continues to be I am. See also Mat 7:29, "for he taught them as one who had authority, and not as their law professors." The Greek words translated "as one who had authority" are, ἐξουσίαν ἔχων [4]exousian, from ek, out of, source, origin, and eimi, I am; and the word ἔχων echoon means to hold or echo; thus, **the teachings of Jesus echo I am!** This is what made his teachings different from the law professors who taught the letter of the law of works, and not the poema, the poetry of the law of life; there are two trees here, the same two trees in the garden of Eden; two systems: the works of the flesh vs. the Tree of Life; the house on the Rock, Deut 32:18, Isa 51:1; thus, our true identity vs. a house on the sand; which is the flesh identity.)*

4:33 And in the synagogue, a man with an unclean, demonic spirit began hollering out loud,

4:34 What do we have in common Jesus of Nazareth!? Did you come to [1]break our hold on people? I know who you are! You are the Holy one of God! *(Literally, "what is there to us and to you?" The word, [1]apollumi, is derived from apo, away from, and luo, to loosen, to undo, to dissolve.*

See Rev 9:11 Their reigning king was the celestial shepherd-messenger of the bottomless pit; his name in Hebrew was [1]Abaddon and in Greek, Apollyon - the One who breaks the bonds! [[1]Abaddon אבדון from abad, to wander away, - we all like sheep have gone astray. He found us and delivered us from our abandonment. He left no stone unturned in seek-

ing and finding every single lost sheep! He went into the most extreme depths of our lost-ness and hell! He is called the Searcher of those who have wandered away! See 2 Cor 2:15, This parade of victory is a public announcement of the defeat of the religious systems and structures based on the law of works. Just like it is in any public game where the victory celebration of the winning team is an embarrassment for the losing team. The death of evil is announced in resurrection life! The word, **apollumi,** *is derived from* **apo,** *away from, and* **luo,** *to loosen, to undo, to dissolve. The message we communicate is a fragrance with an immediate association; to darkness, it is the smell of doom [the death of death] See also my comment on John 3:16. Also 1 John 3:8, Sin's source is a fallen mindset, from the beginning! For this purpose the son of God was revealed! His mission was to undo [*apollumi*] the works of the Devil! The word,* **diabolos,** *from* **dia,** *because of and* **ballo,** *to cast down. Isaiah 54:16])*

4:35 Jesus rebuked him and commanded him to immediately shut up and get out of the man. With that, the man was flung to the ground but not hurt.

4:36 Everyone was shocked and wondering with amazement about the dynamic of this word that charged unclean spirits and they left.

4:37 This conversation continued to resound throughout the entire region and went viral. *(The verb εξεπορευετο ekseporeueto, to spiral out from a specific area, is in the Imperfect Middle Indicative tense, thus, it kept on going forth. The word, ἦχος echos means a sound, noise, like the roar of the sea waves.)*

4:38 When Jesus stood up from the teacher's seat and left the synagogue that day, he went to Simon's house where his mother in law was harassed by a persistent and very severe fever.

4:39 Jesus [1]leaned over her and rebuked the fever and it left her; she immediately got up and prepared a meal for them. *(Luke, the medical man, gives such attention to detail,* **epistas epanō autēs,** *Jesus leaning over her; he pictures Jesus as the kindly sympathetic physician.)*

4:40 At sunset everyone who had family or friends suffering from any kind of disease brought them to him, and he laid his hands on them, one by one, and cured them all. *(It was the end of the Sabbath and carrying anything on the Sabbath was regarded as* *work. See John 5:10. Robertson notes: He heals one by one with the tender touch upon each one. Luke alone gives this graphic detail which was more than a mere ceremonial laying on of hands. Clearly the cures of Jesus reached the physical, mental, and spiritual planes of human nature. He is Lord of life and acted here as Master of each individual case as it was presented to him.)*

4:41 Demons also came out of many crying out, "You are the son of God!" Jesus shut them up. While demons knew that he was the Messiah, he didn't need any devil to promote him.

4:42 It was almost dawn the next day when Jesus finally got to break away into a solitary place where he could spend some time alone. But the multitudes pursued him an when they found him, they just clung to him and wouldn't let him go.

4:43 He said to them, you will have to let me go to the other cities also! I am on a mission to announce the good news of the Kingdom of God to everyone.

4:44 And thus he continued to [1]be what he was commissioned to do, a Herald of the good news in all the synagogues of Judea. *(Again the verb, aen, ην is used; the Imperfect Active of eimi, I am - thus, to continue to be I am!)*

5:1 The crowds were pressing upon him to get close enough to hear him teach the word of God; he was standing on the edge of the shore of Gennesaret. *(The word, λίμνη **limnē**, from λιμήν **limen**, harbor, through the idea of nearness of shore. Gennesaret is also called the sea of Galilee)*

5:2 There were two boats lying against the shore. The sea-folk had already gone out to wash their fishing nets.

5:3 Jesus then, stepped into the boat belonging to Simon and asked him to row out a little from the land; then he sat down and continued teaching from the boat.

5:4 When he paused his teaching, he asked Simon to take them into deep water where they could let down the net for a catch.

5:5 Simon responded, *"*[1]Captain! We've been toiling all through the night, and caught nothing, but [2]mirrored in your word I will let down the net! *(Only Luke uses the word, επιστατα [1]epistata - 7 times in his gospel - Simon announces Jesus the Skipper of his boat! You're the Captain! From now on, you call the shots! Luke again repeats the proposition [2]epi, ἐπὶ δὲ τῷ ῥήματί; at, over against, across - thus, mirrored in your word!)*

5:6 They did this and trapped a massive school of large fish! So large was their haul, that the nets began to tear!

5:7 Then they signalled to their partners in the other boat to come and assist them. When they arrived, they filled both vessels to capacity which almost sank the boats.

5:8 Witnessing this, Simon fell on his knees and began to beg Jesus to leave! "Depart from me Lord, for I am a sinful man!" *(Religion over the years has majored on the subject of sin-consciousness. The moment something goes wrong, guilt trips are empowered. Simon's response surprises after he witnesses the teaching and ministry of Jesus, and a catch that he could not claim any credit for! "Depart from me Lord, for I am a sinful man!" He apparently felt a lot more familiar and comfortable to account the previous night's toil and no success to his own sinfulness! Karma makes so much sense to a religion that makes its money out of paying and returning customers!)*

5:9 These people, who were sea-folk all their lives, have never witnessed a catch like this in their wildest dreams! Simon and everyone there on that day, were totally overcome with awe.

5:10 His partners, James and John, the sons of Zebedee, were equally astonished. Then Jesus said to Simon, You have nothing to fear! From now on you'll likewise be "netting" people alive! *(Zebedee, זבדי Jaweh is my gift. The word, ζωγρέω zogreo, from ζωή Zoe, life; and ἄγρα agra as in 5:4,5 and 5:9, to catch, trap; thus to be netting people alive in order to re-discover Zoe-life!)*

5:11 Then, after bringing their boats to land, they [1]departed from everything that defined them before and followed him. *(Again Luke employs the word ἀφίημι [1]aphiemi, from apo, away from and eimi, I am.)*

5:12 In one of the towns they visited, there was a man in an advanced stage of leprosy, who, seeing Jesus, cast himself at his feet and implored him, "Sir, if you wish, I know that you are able to make me clean."

5:13 And Jesus stretched out his hand and touched him saying, I am delighted to; be clean! And immediately the leprosy left him completely.

5:14 And he gave him strict instruction not to tell anyone, but to go to the priest and offer the oblation according to the law of Moses as proof to people that he is clean. *(Lev 13 and 14.)*

5:15 His fame escalated even more dramatically. Great multitudes crowded together to hear him and be healed of their infirmities.

5:16 But he would often retire secretly into a remote area in prayer.

5:17 Then, one day, while he was teaching, the following dramatic incident happened. There were Pharisees and Scholars of the law also sitting in his audience along with people coming from every village in Galilee and Judea as well as the outskirts of Jerusalem. The very atmosphere was charged with the presence of the Lord to heal. *(See Luke's account of Paul's ministry in Acts 14:1 - "he taught in such a way, that many believed!")*

5:18 Meanwhile, there were people desperately trying to get into the house where Jesus was teaching; they were carrying a man on a bed who suffered from severe convulsions that left him paralyzed. If only they could get him close to where Jesus was teaching. But, because of the crowd they were unable to. *(Dr Luke uses the technical medical term, ος ην παραλελυμενος - hos aen paraleloumenos in the Perfect Passive Participle Tense;*

81

describing a state that exists, as a result of something that happened previously. The man was left paralyzed possibly because of an accident or seizures.)

5:19 Then, having no alternative, they got onto the roof and proceeded to break the roof open by taking the tiles off and then lowering him down on his bed to exactly where Jesus was. *(Peter's house apparently, Mark 2:1. Jesus and everyone in the house obviously heard the noise and witnessed the commotion; now why didn't Jesus interrupt their efforts and spared the house from being damaged by them, with a simple "magic-wand" type of healing? He saw strategic opportunity to use this dramatic event to powerfully reinforce the essence of his mission, which was to dismantle the entire sin consciousness-currency of the religious system of the day.)*

5:20 And when Jesus saw their faith, he said to the man, "Your sins are forgiven!" *(Oh WOW! He just pulled the religious rug out from under their favorite philosophy's feet! Suddenly the Pharisees and law professors felt very vulnerable. Their entire leverage over people are in question. Sin-consciousness is their currency! Remember Simon's response earlier in the chapter! "Depart from me Lord, for I am a sinful man!" Jesus deliberately dismantles this idea! Innocence is our design! This is even before the cross! In order to persuade the human race, Jesus was en-route to give mankind the largest possible platform in the universe to exhibit their authentic worth and reclaim their innocence in his death as our death and in his resurrection as our resurrection!")*

5:21 This triggered immediate controversy. The law professors and Pharisees in the house, were perplexed and whispered under their breath, "This is blasphemy! Who does this man think he is!? Surely, only God has the power to forgive sins!"

5:22 Jesus knew exactly what they were thinking and asked them, "Why do you even reason like this in your hearts?

5:23 To say, your sins are forgiven, instead of, rise up and walk, does not make the one more relevant than the other.

5:24 Now, let me show you the connection here and help you see for yourselves that the son of man has authority on earth to forgive sins!" Jesus then again addressed the paraplegic man saying, "Arise, lift up your pallet and be on your way home!" *(The entire basis of the healing ministry of Jesus is reinforced*

82

in the fact that he came to break the association people had with sin as the cause of sickness - he has come to redeem mankind's innocence! Sickness is not some form of "Karma"! We have nurtured the idea for generations! When she falls in love, Maria von Trapp sings, "For somewhere in my youth or childhood, I must have done something good!" While all along engaging the same reward-based, DIY-Tree-system.)

5:25 The lame man instantly responded, got up, took his bedroll and left for home, magnifying God all the way!

5:26 Everyone were beside themselves with ecstatic joy! Overawed, they continued to praise God, mesmerized with the wonder of the paradox they have just witnessed! *(Luke here, uses the word* **ekstasis** *literally standing outside yourself! Then he uses* **paradoxa,** *which is the only time it's used in the NT. Its modern meaning is, a seemingly contradictory statement which, when investigated may prove to be well founded or true. As we all know, both words are accepted English words today.)*

5:27 With this, Jesus left and on his way noticed a tax collector, Levi; he was at the tax office when Jesus said to him, "Join me on my journey!" *(At the place of toll -* **epi to telōnion** *- the tax-office or custom-house of Capernaum placed here to collect taxes from the boats going across the lake outside of Herod's territory or from people going from Damascus to the coast, a regular caravan route.)*

5:28 He got up, left everything behind and immediately began his new journey with Jesus.

5:29 He then invited Jesus to his house where he prepared a very large banquet to his honor. A great many tax collectors as well as a crowd of people from all walks of life attended the feast. *(Again Luke draws specific attention to the fact that sinners are celebrating their friendship with Jesus - As head of the human race he represents every human life; he mirrors the original blueprint of the life of our design. The most labeled sinners in society were irresistibly attracted to him; what the prostitutes and publicans witnessed in his life, mirrored the redeemed integrity of their own; they knew that what they thought to be their life, was a lie.)*

5:30 Meanwhile, there was a lot of muttering going on by the Pharisees and their law professors - they were obviously not invited to the party and were standing on the outskirts voicing their disgust in what was happening. They then confronted

Jesus' disciples! "Why do you eat and drink with tax collectors and sinners!?" *(Again, Jesus was building on his reputation, See Luke 7:33,34 First you have the Baptist on the stage of your entertainment and he doesn't eat bread or drink any wine - he's into fasting and no parties - and you conclude that he is crazy and most probably tormented by a demon. Then, the son of man is the next actor on your stage, he eats and drinks and you say he is a glutton and drunkard! I mean, look at his friends, they are the scum of society - prostitutes and publicans!)*

5:31 Jesus answered, "Those who are in good health need no physician; the ailing do.

5:32 I didn't come to [1]re-define the self-righteous but those who realize they [2]couldn't get it right by themselves. I came to awaken 'sinners' to recognize their [1]authentic identity mirrored in a complete [3]re-aligned mind" *(I did not come to καλέω [1]kaleo to surname/to identify by name. The word sinner, is the word ἁμαρτωλός [2]hamartolos, from ha, negative or without and meros, portion or form; thus to be without your allotted portion or without form, pointing to a disorientated, distorted and bankrupt identity; the word meros, is the stem of morphe, as in second Corinthians 3:18 the word metamorphe, with form, which is the opposite of hamartia - without form. Sin is to live out of context with the blueprint of one's design; to behave out of tune with God's original harmony. The word μετάνοια [3]metanoia from meta, together with, and, noieō, to perceive with the mind, which suggests an awakening of the mind, a re-alignment of one's reasoning. It has nothing in common with the Latin word paenitentia - where the idea of penance and repentance stems from!)*

noieō, to perceive with the mind. It describes the awakening of the mind to that which is true; a re-alignment of one's reasoning; it is a gathering of one's thoughts, a co-knowing. Faith is not a decision; it is a discovery. It has nothing in common with the Latin word paenitentia - where the idea of penance and repentance stems from!

5:33 Then his critics said to him, "Why would John's disciples frequently fast and make prayerful petitions; just as the followers of the Pharisees do; while those close to you are feasting and drinking?" *(The tradition of fasting and prayers of petition and supplication was forged in the idea of obtaining "leverage" through personal discipline in abstaining from something in order to prove to deity your sincere earnestness and thereby hopefully persuade their favor. This is typical of the sin-conscious-driven currency. Their abstinence was paying for their sins and buying favor from their deity. Also referenced in the incidence with the fisherman, having toiled all night and took nothing! They "fasted" their catch! Then the words of Jesus and the extravagance of his gifts completely disarm them! See my comments in Luke 5:8. Innocence puts religion out of business!*

*Sadly, John's disciples had more in common with the Pharisees than with Jesus. Yet it was he who announced Jesus to be the Lamb of God, who takes away the sins of the world; he saw the heavens open and witnessed the Holy Spirit alighting upon him in the form of a dove and heard the voice of God endorsing the sonship of Jesus. But, instead of becoming the first disciple of Jesus, he continued his own ministry. He continued to preach sin and condemnation as if the Lamb did not really take away the sin of the whole world. The very portion of scripture he proclaimed under the prophetic unction of the Spirit, from Isaiah 40:3, begins with the words, in verse 1 and 2: "Comfort, comfort my people, says your God. Speak tenderly to Jerusalem and cry to her that her warfare is ended and her iniquity is pardoned!" Sadly, the ministry of guilt and condemnation seems to be blind to the good of the gospel. Condemning Herod's lust after his brother's wife landed John in prison. See Luke 3:19,20. Doubt and offence begins to haunt him and from prison he sends his disciples to ask Jesus, "Are you the one who is to come, or shall we look for another?" Jesus answers them, "Go tell John what you see and hear: the blind receive their sight and the lame walk, lepers are cleansed and the deaf hear, and the dead are raised up, and the poor have good news preached to them. And blessed is he who takes no offence at me." Math 11: 2-6. **Whatever offends you neutralizes you!** In the book of Acts, Luke writes about Paul's first visit to Ephesus where he finds disciples of John the Baptist, many years after their leader was murdered. They have never even heard about the Holy Spirit, and were still preaching a doctrine of sin-consciousness. Acts 19: 1-6.)*

5:34 Then Jesus said, "No one is under any obligation to fast when there is a bridal banquet in process! Least of all the sons who are taking care of the bridegroom!

5:35 Yet, there will be days when the bridegroom is taken away from them - in those days they will have an opportunity to fast!" *(Fasting briefly from the sense and awareness of his presence - until he endows them with his fulness and power at Pentecost! See John 16:16 For a brief while I will be absent from your view; then in another* *brief while you will see and know me. Also John 16:20 During this brief time of my apparent absence you will mourn and grieve but while the religious world rejoices, your pain will give birth to joy! John 16:21 The anguish a woman suffers when her hour has come to give birth, is soon forgotten and replaced with delight when another human life is born! John 16:22 Just like with childbirth where joy eclipses the labor pains, so your present sorrow then, will be vanquished and your hearts will erupt in joy when you realize how you captivate my gaze! And no one will be able to take this joy away from you! [Again the word οψομαι is used, from **horaoo**, to look at something with wide open eyes as in gazing at something remarkable! In the mirror reflection of his gaze, we see ourselves and now we know even as we have always been known!] Then, John 14:18 At no time will you be orphaned or abandoned by me; I myself come to abide face to face with you. [I will not be less face to face with you than what I've always been face to face with the Father from the beginning of all eternity. The Holy Spirit does not replace, but reinforces the presence of Jesus and the closeness of the Father. Again, John uses the word [1]**pros**, face to face. See John 1:1])*

5:36 Then Jesus proceeded to illustrate the following point, again using powerful parable-analogies, "No-one would tear off a piece of cloth from a new garment in order to patch-up an old worn-out garment! This will not only spoil the new garment but the patch [1]won't even match the old! *(There is no possible* συμφωνέω [1]**sumphōneō** *between the two. The symphony is lost!)*

5:37 It will be such a waste to pour new wine into old skin bottles - the new wine will burst the old bottles and spill the wine on the ground!

5:38 New wine is stored and preserved in fresh wine skins. Thus both wine and skin are equally treasured.

5:39 Yet, you continue to reason that you are so familiar with the old mindsets that you have no appetite for the new!" *(The point Jesus is reinforcing, is the contrast between two mindset-systems - the old religious system of managing personal behavior and performance, with its sin-conscious currency of judgment and reward vs. the entire new, Messianic message of favor, forgiveness, restored innocence and union with our Bridegroom! Gift-language offends reward-language!)*

6:1 Then, one [1]Sabbath day, while they were walking through a field of ripe wheat, his disciples were plucking and eating the grain they rubbed out in their hands. " (*"[1]And it came to pass on the second Sabbath after the first...or, on the second-first Sabbath! Robertson remarks, There is Western and Syrian [Byzantine] evidence for a very curious reading here which calls this sabbath "secondfirst" -[1]deuteroprōtōi. It is undoubtedly spurious, though Westcott and Hort print it in the margin. The most probable explanation is that a scribe wrote "first" [prōtōi] on the margin because of the sabbath miracle in Luk 6:6-11. Then another scribe recalled Luk 4:31 where a sabbath is mentioned and wrote "second" [deuterōi] also on the margin. Finally a third scribe combined the two in the word deuteroprōtōi that is not found elsewhere. See my comment on Rev 1:8 We have no original manuscript - the thousands of manuscripts we do have are handwritten copies of copies for centuries and, unlike my own commentary notes where I have used italics and brackets, there were no such thing in those days which means this could easily have happened where a scribe's notes became text!*)*

6:2 Again there were some Pharisees around who were offended and asked, "Why do you do what is strictly forbidden on a Sabbath!" *(According to Rabbinical notions, what they did was reaping, threshing, winnowing, and preparing food all at once. Plummer.)*

6:3 Jesus looked them straight in the eyes and said, have you never read what David and his followers did when they were hungry? *(The preposition, **pros** means face to face. Note the force of οὐδὲ: "have you not so much as read?" Or, "have you not read even this?")*

6:4 How he entered God's house and ate the [1]Bread of the Presence and also gave it to his followers! While,according to the law, only the priests were allowed to eat it! *(See Heb 9:2 The Hebrew word, לחם הפנים lechem haPānīm, [1]face bread, or bread of the presence. What happened to us in Christ is according to God's eternal purpose [Bread of the Presence, or Show-bread, in Greek, πρόθεσις [1]prothesis, pre-designed/prophetic purpose] which he has shown in every prophetic pointer and shadow; in the Hebrew tradition the show-bread pointed to the true bread from heaven, the authentic word that proceeded from the mouth of God - Jesus, the incarnate word - sustaining the life of our design. The show-bread pointed towards the daily sustenance of life in the flesh as the ultimate tabernacle of God, realized in the account of Jesus with the two men from Emmaus; their hearts were burning with resonance and faith while he opened the*

Scriptures to them, and then, around the table, their eyes were opened to recognize him as the fulfillment of Scripture, their true meal incarnated [Lk 24:27-31]. Mankind shall not live by bread alone, but by the authentic thought of God; the Word proceeding from his mouth, the original intent, his image and likeness incarnated, revealed, and redeemed in human life. See note to 1 Cor 11:34.

Heb 9:6 In the context of this arrangement the priests performed their daily duties, both morning and evening. [The daily duties included their dress and preparations, baptisms, sacrificial offerings, lighting and trimming, removing the old show-bread and replacing it with fresh bread every Sabbath, and sprinkling the blood of the sin offerings before the veil of the sanctuary.])

6:5 The son of man is not the slave of the Sabbath, he is Master of the Sabbath. *(This is not what the Jews wanted to hear! But Jesus is speaking about a different Sabbath! Just like John reminds us in chapter 2 that he had a different temple in mind; one that he would rebuild in 3 days! And in the next chapter with Nicodemus he points to a different birth; not his mother's womb, but our joint-genesis from above! Then the Samaritan woman in chapter 4 discovers a different well; one that bursts forth from within! So here in chapter 5 Jesus sees a different Sabbath to Jewish sentiment! The Sabbath of God points to his perfect work of both revealing and redeeming his image and likeness in human form. Every Sabbath continues to celebrate the perfection of our Father's work - ¹until ²now! So when Jesus heals people on the Sabbath he is not contradicting it, but endorsing it! Jesus is what the Sabbath is all about! He is the substance of every prophetic shadow! In restoring someone's wholeness, the idea of the original Sabbath is reinforced and not compromised! When God introduced the Sabbath it was always meant to be a prophetic opportunity to celebrate his rest, which was him seeing his perfect work unveiled in us! He continues to invite us to enter into his Rest where we cease from our own works! The announcement, "You shall do NO WORK!" was to remind us again and again that his work is perfect, and we cannot improve on it! You cannot improve on you! You are his workmanship - his masterpiece! The deadly fruit of the "I am not Tree - system" had to be thoroughly uprooted! Hebrews 4:4 [Read the entire chapter 4 in the Mirror] Scripture records the seventh day to be the prophetic celebration of God's perfect work. What God saw satisfied his scrutiny. [Behold, it is very good, and God rested from all his work. Gen 1:31, 2:2. God saw more than his perfect image in Adam, he also saw the Lamb and his perfect work of redemption! "The Lamb having been slain from the foundation of the world." Rev 13:8, "That which has been is now; that which is to be, already has been." Ecc*

3:15. Also 2 Tim 1:9.] Hebrews 4:10 God's rest celebrates his finished work; whoever enters into God's rest immediately abandons his own efforts to compliment what God has already perfected. [The language of the law is "do;" the language of grace is "done."] Faith is God's language; God calls things which are not [visible yet] as though they were. Rom 4:17.)

6:6 The following incident happened on another Sabbath where he was again teaching in the synagogue. In the audience there was a man whose right hand was withered.

6:7 The law professors and Pharisees were watching him insidiously, to see whether he would heal on the Sabbath day. These, typical plaintiffs, were hoping to gather more evidence in building their growing case of [1]accusation against Jesus. *(The word κατήγορος [1]kategoros, a name given to the Devil by the Rabbis, the one whose business is accusation, from kata, downward and agora, to trade.)*

6:8 But Jesus, knowing exactly what they were thinking, told the man with the withered hand to stand up and immediately step into the center of the synagogue. The man did so without hesitation. *(The command, στηθι stethi, step into the center, is in the Aorist Active Imperative tense; this means to get it over and done with immediately - to do so without delay!)*

6:9 Jesus then addressed the plaintiff with this question, "What would be the more acceptable thing to do on a Sabbath, good or bad? To restore a life or to destroy it? *(The rabbis had a rule: Periculum vitae pellit sabbatum. But it had to be a Jew whose life was in peril on the sabbath. The words of Jesus cut to the quick. [Robertson.] Jesus again employs a paradox - while they're plotting to destroy him on a Sabbath, he is about to heal.)*

6:10 He took his time and looked everyone in the eye from the one end of the audience to the other and then spoke to the man, "Stretch out your hand!" He immediately did this and his hand was perfectly restored! *(The word περιβλεψαμενος periblepsamenos is an Aorist Middle Participle - the middle voice giving a personal touch to it all. He looked each one in the eye - all around, from the one end to the other. The verb, εκτεινον ekteinon, stretch out, is again an Aorist Active Imperative - do so without hesitation! Here is a man who was hopelessly incapable of doing what Jesus told him to do, but empowered by the authority of his word, he stretched out his hand!)*

6:11 This infuriated the Pharisees and law professors with extreme rage - their maddened minds were bursting with anger! Immediately they continued plotting their options on how to destroy Jesus. *(The words, επλησθησαν ανοιας eplēsthēsan anoias - means, they were filled to overflowing with madness - literally, anoias from the negative particle α, and νοῦς mind; thus, without mind; they were out of their minds with madness. Dr Luke - also the psychologist here - uses this word to point out how one can no longer reason logically when anger takes over. Only he and Paul uses this word, 2 Tim 3:8,9. We get our word, annoy from anoias, which suggests, that to be annoyed can trigger a dangerous energy which disengages one's logical reasoning!)*

6:12 It was in that time that he again departed into the mountain to engage in prayer - he spent the night there; entwined in the face to face embrace of God. *(He continued all night - ēn dianuktereuōn, this is the Periphrastic Imperfect Active tense, which is only used here in the N.T., but common in the LXX and in late Greek writers. Medical writers used it of whole night vigils. Then Luke employs a phrase that again occurs nowhere else, ἐν τῇ προσευχῇ τοῦ Θεοῦ en tēi proseuchēi tou theou, which is the Objective Genitive - in the prayer of God! The word proseuche, often translated, prayer, as in proseuchomai, from pros, face to face and euche, eu, well done echo - a place of mutual resonance where desires are mirrored. The word euchomai also translates, good wish, or good desire.)*

6:13 The next day he summoned his disciples and designated twelve of them as apostles. *(The word, apostolos, one on assignment, sent out on a mission; an ambassador.)*

6:14 They were Simon, whom he named Peter, and Andrew his brother; James and John; Philip and Bartholomew;

6:15 Matthew and Thomas; James of Alphaeus and Simon called the Zealot;

6:16 Judas of James, and Judas, the man of Kerioth, who became traitor. *(Iscariot was not his surname, but literary means the man of Kerioth, a small town a few miles south of Hebron. Judas was not Galilean like the rest of the disciples, but a Judean and seemed to have struggled more than any of them to see the significance of the mirror likeness of Jesus as defining his true sonship. See reference to Kerioth in Amos 2:2 and then, in Amos 2:5, "because they sell the righteous for silver!" Also John 6:71 and John 7:1; then, John 17:12.)*

Here is a portion of a most beautiful poem about Judas, written by my friend Dusty Harrison - see the entire poem here: https://www.facebook.com/556536215/posts/10155865183711216/

After his suicide was accomplished, Judas lifted up his eyes in a black flame of darkness.

He remembered his betrayal and his defection... his silver thrown... the eyes of his master as he kissed him in the garden.

His thoughts turned in his pain to the words of his master as he spoke them...

Parables of lost things and sorrow filled him...

The lost sheep... wandering off and leaving his flock... and the goodness of the Shepherd leaving the ninety-nine and going after the one... returning with it laid on his shoulders rejoicing...

The woman's lost coin as she searched diligently, sweeping frantically and finally finding it.. and rejoicing and throwing a party for her friends because what had been lost was found and had never lost its value...

The lost Son... and his good Father.

The boy wasting his inheritance...

feeding pigs and longing to return home...

Lost son... the son of perdition.

I have lost none but the son of perdition, he remembered... that the scriptures may be fulfilled... and then...

The skies above both hell and paradise were split... as light poured in... the light that dwarfed even that of paradise... a shout of triumph rained down to him...

and in paradise, a man appeared... a lamb as it had been slain stood with a thief who was jumping and shouting for joy...

The black flame turned to red and yellow...

and the great gulf between paradise was filled with blood like water and across the gulf came the lamb walking on the blood like water... as he approached, the darkness receded and he saw that The Father and Spirit were standing behind him... then his master came close and kissed him on the cheek...

and Judas wept...)

6:17 He then came down from the mountain with them and stood in an open plain where a crowd of his followers and a large multitude of people were gathering; they were coming from all over Judea and Jerusalem as well as the coastal regions of Tyre and Sidon.

6:18 They were there, [1]determined to hear Jesus teach and to be [2]healed of their infirmities. Also those who were harassed by unclean spirits were amongst them and they too were healed. *(Luke always connects Jesus healing ministry with his teaching. As in his account of Paul's ministry in the book of Acts, "Paul preached in such a way, that many believed... Acts 14:1; also on another occasion in Acts 14:8,9, ...while he was teaching, he saw a man's face lit up with faith...!*

This is such a different attitude to the law professors and Pharisees who sat in the same audience, with frowns on their foreheads!

They were there, [1]determined to hear ακουσαι from akouō to hear; which is an Aorist Active Infinitive; Greek Infinitives could have either a Present or Aorist form. The contrast between the two forms has more to do with aspect than with time. The Present Infinitive is used to express progressive or imperfective aspect. It pictures the action expressed by the verb as being in progress. The Aorist Infinitive however does not express progressive aspect. It presents the action expressed by the verb as a determined, completed unit with a beginning and end. Thus, they had their minds made up! They were going to hear with understanding and be healed! The next verb, ιαθηναι iathenai, is also an Aorist Infinitive, this time in the Passive voice of ιάομαι [2]iaomai to heal, from ιαίνω iaínō, "to warm". Of the 29 times this word is used in the NT, Luke uses it 17 times - as medical man he is interested to know how someone feels who experiences the healing touch of Jesus! This is amazing! Also in my own experience, when praying with people, I have had people testify that they felt heat moving through their bodies or in the affected areas! I believe, that while reading the Mirror Bible, unveiled understanding comes to you and faith and healing happens! I do not imply that someone has to "feel" the heat in order to be healed! Many times healing happens without any "feeling"!)

6:19 Everyone in the crowd was pressing in to touch him, because power was surging from him and he healed them all, one by one. *(The word, άπτομαι haptomai, means to cling to; attach oneself to; from άπτω haptō, to be kindled! Then the sentence, δύναμις παρ'* αὐτοῦ ἐξήρχετο - **dunamis para auto eksercheto, - para,** closest possible proximity of nearness - out of his innermost being. Then, **kai iāto pantas -** with ιατο is in the Imperfect Middle voice, he kept on healing every single one; the Middle voice giving a personal touch to it all.)

At this pivotal point of Jesus' ministry, he continues to dismantle the entire philosophy of a religion based upon the typical Deuteronomy chapter 28 model! The idea of blessings and curses, as defining human life, is challenged to the core! One can only imagine the stories of horror proportions represented in the masses of diseased and tormented people who came to be healed by Jesus. Yet Luke makes no reference whatsoever to the degree of need or the merit of any individual case that qualifies someone to be healed. At no point does Jesus encourage anyone to first "say a sinners prayer", or perhaps first show remorse and confess or tell their sad stories of abuse etc. Neither did he make any appointments for further, extended counselling sessions. Yet, Jesus' healing ministry was not based on the "Magic wand" style; he always taught and healed! See Luke 5:5 & 17. See also my commentary note in chapter 6:18.

Now follows, **The Beatitudes**, a word, connected to this teaching of Jesus by the Eastern church fathers in 15th century, from the Latin beātitūdō, from beātus "happy, fortunate" + tūdō, indicating a state or condition; thus, a state of utmost bliss!

6:20 Finally, having concluded his healing of the multitudes, Jesus lifted up his eyes and spoke to his followers, "To be [2]reduced to the most extreme state of poverty, does not define you. Disaster is not the fruit of [1]fate or karma [performance-based religion]**! The [1]blessing of knowing, that the Kingdom of God [3]belongs to you personally, and that it is oozing from you, is the essence of your wellbeing and identity!"** (The word translated blessed, μακαριοι [1]**makarioi**, stems from μη, mey not, and **keyr**, κηρ, fate! Fate has no say here! The word, πτωχός [2]**ptōchos**, poverty; bankruptcy; reduced to a crouching, beggarly state - from πτωσσω, to tremble, or shrink with fear. Associated with judgment. The word, ὑμέτερος [3]**humeteros**, proceeding from you; belonging to you!

Sadly, just like Simon's religious response, "Depart from me Lord, for I am a sinful man", the law professors and Pharisees were more interested in their question of, "Why was the boy born blind!?" John 9. Was it his own sin, or perhaps "a generational curse" inherited from his parents!? The concept of fate has been predominant in Greek/Roman myth and the driving force for most of their stories. In the Hebrew mind, מזל טוב mazal tov, good fortune, plays a major role, but it is always connected to their entire performance-based philosophy and religion.

See Romans 1:17 Herein lies the secret of the power of the Gospel; there is no good news in it until the righteousness of God is revealed! The dynamic of the gospel is the revelation of God's faith as the only valid basis for our belief. The Prophets wrote in advance about the fact that God believes that righteousness reveals the life of our design. "Righteousness by his [God's] faith defines life." [Habakkuk 2:4]

[The gospel is the revelation of the righteousness of God; it unveils how the Father, Son and Spirit succeeded to put mankind right with themselves. It is about what God did right, not what Adam did wrong. The good news reveals how God's righteousness rescued the life of our design and redeemed our innocence. Mankind's futile efforts to obey moral laws have failed them miserably - the Good News shifts the emphasis away from mankind's failure and condemnation to highlight what it was that God accomplished in Jesus Christ on mankind's behalf! "Look away [from the law of works] unto Jesus; he is the Author and finisher of faith." [Hebrews 12:1]. The language of the old written code was, "Do in order to become! The language of the new is, "Be, because of what was done!" Instead of do, do, do, it's done, done, done! It is God's faith to begin with; it is from faith to faith, and not our good or bad behavior; we are not defined by our performance or circumstances. Paul refers here to Habakkuk 2:4, "The just shall live by his [God's] faith." Habakkuk sees a complete new basis to mankind's standing before God! Instead of reading the curse when disaster strikes, he realizes that the Promise out-dates performance as the basis to mankind's acquittal. The curse is taken out of the equation! Gal 3:13. Deuteronomy 28 would no longer be the motivation or measure of right or wrong behavior! Instead of righteousness as a reward to mankind's efforts to obey the law, Habakkuk celebrates God's righteousness based on God's belief, in the face of apparent disaster, represented in the evidence of all the curses mentioned in Deuteronomy 28! He sings, "Though the fig trees do not blossom, nor fruit be on the vines, the produce of the olive fails and the fields yield no food, the flock be cut off from the fold and there be no herd in the stalls, yet I will rejoice in the Lord, I will joy *in the God of my salvation. God, the Lord, is my strength; he makes my feet like hinds' feet, he makes me tread upon my high places." [Habakkuk 3:17-19 RSV]. It is interesting to note that Habakkuk -* חבקוק *chăbaqqûq, was possibly the son of the Shunammite woman and her husband who hosted the Prophet Elisha. They could not have children, until Elisha declared that in a year's time she would embrace -* חבק *chabaq - a child! When the child grew up to be a young man, he died of sunstroke [fate or karma!?] and Elisha stretched himself over the boy and mirror-embraced the dead child, face to face and the boy came back to life.* חבקוק *Chabaqquq is a double embrace - it is the prophetic picture of our mirror-resurrection together with Christ! If anyone knew that righteousness was not by works, but by God's faith, it was Habakkuk!])*

6:21 From [1]now on, the idea of fate or any sense of judgment when you are faced with famine, is no longer relevant! Since you are blessed with a brand new reference of a far greater reality, where you are abundantly sustained and [2]fully satisfied in lush green pastures! Your reason for weeping, is now transformed into blissful laughter and ecstatic joy! *(Luke adds the adverb* ννν *[1]nun "now" after "famished in famine" and again after "weep." He thus sharpens the contrast of this new reality as reference to this place of bliss. Fully satisfied, χορτασθησεσθε from χορτάζω [2]chortazō as in animal fodder. See Psalm 23, "He makes me lie down in green pastures!" Luke is reminded of Paul's testimony in Phil 4:12, I am not defined by abuse or abundance! It might be a different day and a different place, but the secret remains the same; whether I am facing a feast or a fast, a fountain or famine. Phil 4:13 In every situation I am strong in the one who empowers me from within to be who I am!)*

6:22 Your blissful state remains uninterrupted when, because of your association with me as the son of man, people hate, de-friend, gossip, block and exclude you, or even slander and embarrass you by dragging your name through the mud, making you out to be somebody evil! Your social standing and recognition is no longer based on how popular you are in the typical religious world.

6:23 Hey, instead of sulking about it, [1]click your heels and do a happy dance! You are [2]tapped into heaven's currency and cannot be bought! You are surrounded by a cloud of witnesses! These religious leaders, who are so stoked on their currency of condemnation and judgment are the very same fanatics who

murdered you fathers, the prophets who saw my day! *(Leap for joy σκιρτήσατε [1]skirtēsate, an old verb used in LXX, but only in Luke in the N.T. The word, μισθός misthos, dues paid for work.)*

The blessings of the beatitudes are sharply contrasted here with the sigh of sadness!

6:24 [1]Sigh! How [2]sad to think that the wealth you accumulated by your own toil, is not the [3]true [4]reflection of what you're worth! *(The word [1]plēn denotes a vivid contrast. The word, [2]ouai as in oua, is a sigh of bewilderment -Oh! - Woe! The word, [3]apechō means, a receipt in full, as the papyri show. Then, παράκλησις [4]paraklēsis from para, closest possible association, and kaleo, to surname; to define identity. Thus, making your "wealth"to be proof of your success in keeping the law, the official receipt; the document that defines and credits your successful attempts to justify yourself according to the law of works.)*

6:25 Oh my, oh my! While you might be convinced [1]for the moment, that you are [2]most fully content with your diet of legalism, you will soon realize how famished you actually are! What a shame! Here you are, sneering with laughter while the same things you laugh about now, will make you weep with grief! *(The word, εμπεπλησμενοι from [2]empiplēmi, en + πλεῖστος pleistos the very extreme/most satisfied. Again Luke employs the adverb νυν [1]nun "now", twice, as in Luk 6:21, in vivid contrast between the two scenarios.)*

6:26 Oh, it is such a waste of time! While, trying your best to be in everyone's good books - you are revelling in exactly the same flattery your fathers were giving the false prophets!

Now, just to reinforce the fact that he is not attacking people in the above woes, he introduces the earth-shattering extravagance of the agape of God! This is the same agape Paul celebrates in 1 Corinthians 13; the kind, that keeps no record of wrong!

Jesus is not, as most translations of the above passage would suggest, telling the law professors and Pharisees that God's gonna get them and that they're all gonna burn in hell for this! He is exposing their evil mindsets that will most certainly perish! See my notes on the Lake of Fire in Rev 19.)

6:27 For those of you who are really hearing me, allow me to give this conversation [1]another title! "What it means to discover the

extravagant extent of Agape!" Yes, you are challenged to love the most unlikely - your enemies! Do things that will be to the best advantage of those who despise you! *(The words [1]allos and heteros are both usually translated as "another" in English. Yet allos means "another of the same kind" and heteros means "another of a different type".)*

6:28 Speak well of those who curse you. Pray for those who threaten and slander you.

6:29 If someone violently attacks you, then let him have his way! If you get punched on the jaw, then stand a bit closer in case he wants to hit you again! If he grabs your robe let him have your undergarment too!

6:30 Give to everyone who begs from you. And don't demand anything back if someone takes you for a ride! *[The idiom means, if someone cheats you or steals from you.]*

6:31 The way you treat others, mirrors exactly how you expect people to treat you.

6:32 To only love those who love you, is not what grace is all about! Your regular sinner lives by that rule!

6:33 Grace is not about rewarding a good deed with an equally good one! Even those who are [1]out of sync with their true identity do that. *(Again, the word, hamartōlos - traditionally translated as a sinner; from ha, negative or without, and meros, out of sync with their true identity.)*

6:34 If you lend money to those you expect to receive a return from, then what's grace got to do with it - sinners do the same.

6:35 What I am talking about is a life of [1]total contrast! There is no ways that a life ruled by religious legalism can match this! For starters, love your enemies! Do good and lend to those where there is no chance they'll pay you back! Tapping into heavenly dimension-realities beats living by the rules of the earthly realm of personal performance by far! Your son-ship-likeness, is mirrored in the Most High; he is your Source. He is [2]kindness in person, to the [3]un-christlike *[the unkind]* and to those trapped in the [4]typical lifestyle of hardships labors and annoyances! He embarrasses us with his [2]generosity when we least expect it and are at our worst! *([1]plen, moreover; in total contrast. He is χρηστος [2]chrestos kind, generous - closely associated to the word christos - Christ to the αχαριστους [3]achrestous from the particle, a, without and chrestos; και πονηρους [4]ponerous; often translated evil; to be full of hardships labor and annoyances.)*

6:36 Mirror your Father's compassion. *(The Jewish Zohar and the Talmud express the Divine Being by no other name, than "the Merciful"; רחמן rachman compassionate; merciful אמר רחמנא)*

6:37 Cultivate the [1]habit not to judge anyone! [2]Mirrored in the Father's mercy, you are never judged! Neither see anyone contrary to our shared likeness - since our equal participation in our Father's attributes, is [3]never in question! By setting someone else free from their obligation, you will be setting yourself free - the burden will fall off your shoulders! *("He that judges his neighbor according to the balance of righteousness, or innocence, they judge him according to righteousness." [John Gill - T. Bab. Sabbat, fol. 127. 2.] The Present Imperative in κρινετε [1]krinete, καταδικαζετε and απολυετε apolete, suggests to be in the habit of doing it. The Aorist Passive Subjunctive in κριθητε krithete and καταδικασθητε katadikasthete, suggests inevitable fulfillment. Therefore, our equal participation in his attributes is a given! The double negative ou mē, emphasizes definite certainty - never. The word, καταδικαζετε katadikasthete, often translated, condemned, means, contrary to our shared likeness kata against; δίκη dikay, two parties finding likeness in each other - the stem for the word, righteousness, dikaiosune - where Dikay reminds of the Greek goddess of Justice by the same name, typically portrayed holding a scale of balances in her hand. The word, απολυετε from apoluo, to release someone. See 2 Cor 6:14,15.)*

6:38 Gift language beats reward language by far! This is the [1]mirror-measure! Your giving reflects your source - a good measure, pressed down, shaken together, running over, will they pour into your laps! *(The word, [1]antimetrēthēsetai, from anti, over against, mirror, and metrē, measure. Into your bosom - eis ton kolpon humōn - the fold of the wide upper garment bound by the girdle made a pocket in common use. Remember, you mirror your Father's compassion. And with what measure you mete, it shall be measured to you again. This was a common proverb among the Jews; it is sometimes delivered out thus, מדה כנגד מדה, "measure against measure" John Gill.)*

6:39 Then Jesus proceeded to illustrate the following point, again using parable-analogies: "Imagine a blind person trying

to guide another blind. They will both fall into the same pothole.

6:40 An apprentice does not compete with his instructor. But once he is fully equipped, he mirrors his teacher. *(The word* καταρτίζω *katartizō means, to be fully restored; fitly joined together in perfect harmony.)*

6:41 Talking about judgment, why pretend that you are trying to help your brother remove the splinter out of his eye, when you've got a log in your own!

6:42 Don't be a hypocrite! By drawing attention to something small in your brother's life, you pretend that your life's all sorted out! Get help first, then you'll be so much better equipped to assist your brother!

6:43 A healthy tree produces healthy fruit. If the fruit is no good, there is something wrong with the tree.

6:44 Every tree is identified by its particular fruit; you don't expect figs to grow on a thorn tree, nor a bunch of grapes on a bramble bush.

6:45 In the same way, a good person will bring forth amazing treasures of goodness from the storehouse of their hearts; while a man with a hidden agenda, will not be able to hide the effect of his evil influence. One's conversation exhibits whatever it is that has your full attention and captivates your gaze!

6:46 I'm not teaching you these things to hand out certificates! Calling me, Master and Teacher means nothing - it's all about mirroring my word in your life.

6:47 Let me illustrate what it's like for any individual who follows me, hears my words and fully engages the effect of the message.

6:48 It is like building a storm-proof house. So, this person dug beyond the surface layers, and continued to excavate until solid rock was found. And the foundation of the house was laid upon that rock. Then, one-day, there was a massive cloudburst; the water began to rise and a river came down in flood until it burst its banks in a torrent and broke against the house with full force. Yet, it's intensity did not even shake the structure. The secret is, that this house shares the same strength of the rock, because of the depth of its foundation.

6:49 But, someone who only hears my words casually, without engaging it's message, is like a person who builds a house on the surface, without any foundation; then, when the storm struck and the river burst its banks, the house was swept along! To sit in the same audience with an indifferent attitude, is such a great loss! *(It's not the size of the storm, but it's the connection with the rock that makes all the difference. It's about engaging a rock-solid foundation.*

See Deut 32:4, "Ascribe greatness to our God, the Rock! His work is perfect and all his ways are just! A God of faithfulness, righteous and upright is he." Deut 32:18, "But you were unmindful of the Rock that begot you, and forgot the God who gave you birth." Also Isa 51:1, "Look to the Rock from which you were hewn, the quarry from which you were dug!"

*Jesus asks the most important question in the Bible "Who do people say, that I, the son of man am?" Then he asked his followers, "Who do you say that I am?" The Rock foundation of the Ekklesia that Jesus is both the Architect and Master-builder of, is the unveiling of the Father! The son of man [Rev 1:13] is the son of God! Blessed are you, Simon, son of Jonah! [Bar Jonah, his surname identity] Flesh and blood did not reveal this to you, but My Father! I say, you are Rock, a chip [**petros**] of the old Block [**petra**]! And upon this revelation, that the son of man is the son of God, I will build my Ekklesia and the gates of Hades will not prevail against it. Matthew 16:13-19. **Ekklesia** from **ek**, origin and **kaleo**, to surname; original identity. **Hades**, from **ha**, negative particle, and **eido** to see. In a walled city, the gates are the most strategic point - if the gates are disengaged, the city is taken! Thus, the blindfold mode of mankind's forgotten identity, will not prevail against you!*

See James 1:22 Give the word your undivided attention; do not underestimate yourself. Make the calculation. There can only be one logical conclusion: your authentic origin is mirrored in the word. You are God's poem; let his voice make poetry of your life!

James 1:23 Anyone who hears the word, sees the face of their birth, as in a mirror! The difference between a mere spectator and a participator is that both of them hear the same voice and perceive in its message the face of their own genesis reflected there;

James 1:24 they realize that they are looking at themselves, but for the one it seems just too good to be true; this person departs [back to the old way of seeing himself] and immediately forgets what manner of person they are; never giving another thought to the one they saw there in the mirror.

James 1:25 The other is [1]mesmerized by what they see; [2]captivated by the effect of a law that frees a person from the obligation to the old written code that restricted one to their own efforts and willpower. No distraction or contradiction can dim the impact of what is seen in the mirror concerning the law of perfect [3]liberty [the law of faith] that now frees one to get on with the act of living the life [of their original design.] They find a new [3]spontaneous lifestyle; the poetry of practical living. (The law of perfect liberty is the image and likeness of God revealed in Christ, now redeemed in mankind as in a mirror. Look deep enough into that law of faith that you may see there in its perfection a portrait that so resembles the original that he becomes distinctly visible in the spirit of your mind and in the face of every person you behold. I translated the word, [1]parakupto, as mesmerized, from para, a preposition indicating close proximity, originating from, denoting the point from which an action originates, intimate connection, and kupto, to bend; to stoop down to view at close scrutiny; [2]parameno, to remain captivated under the influence of; meno, to continue to be present. The word often translated as freedom, [3]eleutheria, means to be without obligation; spontaneous.

So, what does it mean to build your house upon the rock? It is all about discovering your authentic identity in Christ and not in flesh, which frees one to now live your life from who you are in Christ [Grace] and not who you are in Adam [law of works]! It is the difference between a display window and a mirror - living "from", rather than, "towards".

2 Cor 3:16 The moment anyone [1]returns to the Lord the veil is gone! [The word, [1]epistrepho means to return to where we've wandered from; "we all like sheep have gone astray." Jesus is God unveiled in human form. [Col 1:15] Also 1 Pet 2:25 You were completely vulnerable, just like sheep roaming astray without direction or protection, but now you have returned and are restored to the shepherd and Guardian of your souls! And 1 Pet 1:17.

2 Cor 3:17 The Lord and the Spirit are one; his Lordship sanctions our freedom. A freedom from rules chiselled in stone to the voice of our redeemed design echoing in our hearts!

2 Cor 3:18 Now, we all, with new understanding, see ourselves in him as in a mirror. The days of window-shopping are over! In him every face is unveiled. In gazing with wonder at the blueprint of God displayed in human form, we suddenly realize that we are looking into a mirror, where every feature of his image articulated in Christ is reflected within us! The Spirit of the Lord engineers this radical transformation; we are led from an inferior mind-set to the revealed endorsement of our authentic identity.])

7:1 All these words were recorded first hand by the people who heard him and when he concluded his teachings, he returned to Capernaum.

7:2 Meanwhile, a slave who was highly valued by his master, was critically ill and dying. He was the servant of a Roman officer, in command of a hundred soldiers.

7:3 Having heard about Jesus, he commissioned some of the Jewish Elders to implore Jesus to come and heal his servant.

7:4 They did so and urged Jesus to come promptly explaining that the Centurion was a very worthy man.

7:5 He loved their nation and even sponsored the building of their Synagogue.

7:6 Jesus immediately joined them and were already near the place when friends of the Centurion met them with this message from the officer saying, "Lord, please do not trouble yourself, I am not competent for you to come under my roof!

7:7 I do not even count myself worthy to come and meet you personally; only speak a word and [1]heal my child! *(For the word iaomai, see commentary note in Luke 6:18.)*

7:8 I too am a man positioned under authority; and have soldiers under me - I would say to one, go and he goes and to another, come and he comes and to my servants, do this and they do!" *(This man understands that just as he represents an authority with the muscle to endorse what he does, so that soldiers or slaves would instantly obey his command, even though they might be physically taller or even stronger than himself; when he speaks, Caesar speaks!)*

7:9 Jesus was pleasantly surprised to hear this! He turned to the crowd of people following him saying, "Wow! I have never found this brand of faith anywhere in Israel."

7:10 And on their return to the house of the Centurion, those who were sent to inform Jesus, found the servant in perfect health.

7:11 The following day he was on his way to Nain with his disciples and a large crowd.

7:12 As they approached the city gate, they encountered a local crowd of people in a funeral procession. They were to bury a boy who was the only child of a widow.

7:13 When the Lord saw her, he was moved with compassion and said to her, "Do not weep!"

7:14 As he approached, he touched the stretcher upon which the dead boy laid and the bearers stopped. He then spoke to the boy, "Young man, awake!"

7:15 The boy sat up and began to speak! And Jesus returned him to his mother.

7:16 Everyone was awestruck and began to magnify God and said, a great prophet has emerged in our midst! We are in God's [1]gaze! (*[1]επεσκεψατο from epi, continual influence upon and skopos, scope; view.*)

7:17 And the ripple effect of this word concerning Jesus, spread throughout Judea and beyond.

7:18 The disciples of John the Baptist told him about all these reports. (*Instead of being overwhelmed with joy, John's response immediately betrays that his personal predicament has completely blurred his focus.*)

7:19 John then, sent two of them to go and ask Jesus, "Are you the one who is to come, or shall we continue to look out for another?" (*Offense converts belief into doubt!*)

7:20 So they went to Jesus and asked him.

7:21 With them watching him, Jesus continued his therapy of healing and cured many people who were suffering from all kinds of diseases as well as those tormented by unclean spirits. He also restored sight to many that were blind.

7:22 Jesus then answered the two disciples, "Now go and tell John what you have seen and heard; the blind see and the lame walk; lepers are cleansed and the deaf hear and the dead are raised and the starving have good news proclaimed to them.

7:23 And tell him, not to allow [1]the idea of fate or judgment to rob him of the bliss of knowing who he is and what he has in me. Offence is a [2]snare. (*See Luke 6:20 The word translated blessed,* μακαριοι *[1]makarioi, stems from* μη, *mey not, and keyr,* κηρ, *fate! Fate has no say here! Don't allow the question, "Why am I suffering like this?" to rob you of your unction and mission! The word,* σκανδαλιζω *[2]skandalizo used here, has the double notion of to trip up and ensnare.*)

See Luke 5:33 Sadly, John's disciples had more in common with the Pharisees than with Jesus. Yet it was he who announced Jesus to be the Lamb of God, who takes away the sins of the world; he saw the heavens open and witnessed the Holy Spirit alighting upon him in the form of a dove and heard the voice of God endorsing his sonship. But, instead of becoming the first disciple of Jesus, he continued his own ministry. He continued to preach sin and condemnation as if the Lamb did not really take away the sin of the whole world. The very scripture he proclaimed in the prophetic unction of the Spirit, from Isaiah 40:3, begins with the words, in verse 1 and 2: "Comfort, comfort my people, says your God. Speak tenderly to Jerusalem and cry to her that her warfare is ended and her iniquity is pardoned!" Sadly, the ministry of guilt and condemnation seems to be blind to the good of the gospel. Condemning Herod's lust after his brother's wife landed John in prison. See Luke 3:19,20. Doubt and offence begins to haunt him and from prison he sends his disciples to ask Jesus, "Are you the one who is to come, or shall we look for another?" Jesus answers them, "Go tell John what you see and hear. And blessed is he who takes no offence in me." Whatever offends you neutralizes you! In the book of Acts, Luke writes about Paul's first visit to Ephesus where he finds disciples of John the Baptist, many years after their leader was murdered. They have never even heard about the Holy Spirit, and were still preaching a doctrine of sin-consciousness. Acts 19: 1-6.

*Also Luke 3:18 And so, with many more words of encouragement John continued to proclaim these amazing good tidings of mankind's redeemed identity and innocence, to the crowds. [The word **parakaleo**, here translated as our joint-genesis, is so key to this sentence of Luke! Sadly, most translations read judgment and exhortation in this beautiful word! And yet they translate **parakletos** as the Comforter elsewhere! The word, **para**, alongside, closest possible proximity of nearness; and **kaleo**, to identify by name, to surname. Also, kinsman; intimate companion. See Rom 12:8, "...just be there alongside someone to remind them of their true identity." 1 Thessalonians 5:11 Continue, as you so eloquently do, to edify one another by cultivating the environment of your close association in your joint-genesis.]*

*Luke 3:19 Later on in his career, John [sadly] also began to voice a strong political opinion by [1]speaking out against the Tetrarch, Herod for his many evils and also because he married his own sister-in-law, Herodias. [The word, [1]**elegcho** means to refute, to point to the evidence as proof. This kind of preaching does not change someone's life! See my commentary note and rendering of 2 Tim 3:16, ...In many fragments of* *prophetic thought, God would heap up the evidence as proof [elegcho] of his purpose to raise fallen mankind up to be co-elevated with him, standing tall like a mountain-monument! The little stone that was cut out by no human hand is destined to strike that image of vanity and piety on its feet of iron and clay, to remove every trace of the substitute, man-made self-image with its glorious head of golden glitter and its silvery bust and bronze body. The stone will become in its place a Rock that fills the whole earth; the true image and likeness of God, restored and revealed in ordinary human life. [Dan 2:32-35.] "And the ends of the earth shall remember and return to the Lord!" Psalm 22:27.]*

Luke 3:20 This, was also the end of John's ministry and lead to his imprisonment and early death. [I said, sadly, since John's initial focus and voice pointed boldly to the Lamb of God, taking away the sins and distortions of the entire world! Having pointed him out, one would have imagined John to be one of the first disciples of Jesus, but later his disciples had more in common with the Pharisees than with Jesus! They would be fasting and praying with the Pharisees while Jesus' disciples were feasting and drinking with sinners and prostitutes!

Many gifted people and their ministries have likewise "lost their heads" by becoming side-tracked into politics and philosophies.])

7:24 When John's messengers left, Jesus addressed the crowd concerning John, asking them, "So what was it that attracted your attention to him when he emerged from the wilderness? Was he just a reed shaken in the wind? Someone with a new flavor of thought, or a fresh philosophical opinion perhaps? *(Jesus doesn't want John's imprisonment and offence, which everyone now witnessed, in his doubting whether he indeed was the Messiah, to distract from the relevance and significance of his profound, prophetic ministry!*

For a better understanding of the idiom of, a reed shaken in the wind, see Jesus' conversation with Nicodemus in John 3:8, We can observe the effect the wind has and hear its sound whenever it touches objects - yet those objects do not define the wind; it comes and goes of its own accord - if life was not born out of spirit in the first place, it would not be possible to detect spirit influence at all! We are spirit-compatible by design! [Spirit is our origin; not our mother's womb!] See 2 Cor 3:3, The fact that you are a Christ-Epistle shines as bright as day! This is what our ministry is all about. The Spirit of God is the living ink. Every trace of the Spirit's influence on the heart is what gives permanence to this conversation. We are not talking law-language here; this is more dynamic and permanent than letters chiseled in stone. This conversation is embroidered in your inner consciousness. [It is the life of your design that grace echoes within you!])

7:25 Was it perhaps his weird dress that attracted your attention? His apparel was certainly not the latest, fine fashion, worn in a king's palace or any place representing the opulence of someone's importance and success. *(People would naturally be drawn to hear what someone has to say, judging by his royal dress-code, as obviously representing the King's palace and authority. Jesus is deliberately pointing to a different kingdom and source of attraction here.)*

7:26 So, what you encountered in the wilderness must have been the real deal - a real prophet? I tell you, indeed, he was a prophet and exceedingly more relevant than any prophet you could ever have imagined!

7:27 He is the one Isaiah wrote about! "Behold, I have sent my messenger to represent my [1]voice and resolve in turning the wilderness into a highway!" *(The word, πρόσωπον [1]prosōpon, my face - my immediate resolve and presence. See Luke 3:4-6.)*

7:28 John is the most significant of all prophets [1]ever born of a woman; yet, in the kingdom of God, the seemingly [2]least significant are even more relevant than John's prophetic status according to the flesh! *(See my comment above in verse 24, [1]Life begins in God, not our mother's womb. What is even more important than John and his present predicament, or even his prophetic status, is the content and effect of his message and mission, which was [2]to point mankind to their authentic origin and innocence; about to be redeemed by the Lamb of God! In the context of this moment within the entire prophetic calendar of God, John is the most relevant voice! Just like his miraculous birth, we too, pre-date our conception in the womb! The Logos is sourced face to face with God; so are we! We began in the same thought! Jeremiah 1:5 - I knew you before I fashioned you in the womb!*

John's response from prison surely must have reminded Luke of his many travels with Paul and what Paul wrote to Timothy in 2 Tim 1:8, Do not let my imprisonment make you feel embarrassed about the testimony of Christ, or your association with me! We are partners in the afflictions of the gospel and also in the intensity of God's power! We experience a constant download of power in the midst of affliction! 2 Tim 1:9 He rescued the integrity of our original design and revealed that we have always been his own from the beginning, even before time was. This has nothing to do with anything we did to qualify or disqualify ourselves. We are not talking religious good works or karma here. Jesus unveils grace to be the eternal intent of God! Grace celebrates our pre-creation innocence and now declares our redeemed union with God in Christ Jesus. Titus 1:2 This is the life of the ages that was anticipated for generations; the life of our original design announced by the infallible resolve of God before time or space existed. [Mankind's union with God is the original thought that inspired creation. There exists a greater dimension to eternity than what we are capable of defining within the confines of space and time! God's faith anticipated the exact moment of our redeemed union with him for all eternity!]

*See 1 Peter 1:10 This salvation which you now know as your own, is the theme of the prophetic thought; this is what intrigued the Prophets' minds for generations and became the object of their most diligent inquiry and scrutiny. 1 Pet 1:11 In all of their conversation there was a constant quest to determine who the Messiah would be, and exactly when this will happen. They knew with certainty that it was the spirit of Christ within them pointing prophetically and giving testimony to the sufferings of the Christ and the subsequent glory. 1 Pet 1:12 It was revealed to them that this glorious grace message that they were communicating pointed to a specific day and person beyond their own horizon and generation; they saw you in their prophetic view! This heavenly announcement had you in mind all along! They proclaimed glad tidings to you in advance, in the Holy Spirit, commissioned from heaven; the celestial shepherd-messengers themselves longed to gaze deeply into its complete fulfillment. [Peter uses the word, **anaggello**, where the preposition, **ana**, points upward to the source of the announcement.] 1 Pet 1:13 How amazing is that! Jesus is what the Scriptures are all about; and you are what Jesus is all about! Now wrap your minds around that! This unveiling is what tied up all the loose ends that would trip you and frustrate your seamless transition from the old to the new! The revelation of Jesus is no longer a future expectation! Do not allow the old mindset of a future tense glory to intoxicate you and distract you from the relevance of this moment! Stop pointing to a future Messiah! Jesus is who the Prophets pointed to! You are the fruit of his sufferings; you are the glorious resurrection generation! Fully engage your minds with the consequence of this grace in the revelation of Jesus Christ! He completes your every expectation! [The word **anazosamenoi**, to gird up, is an Aorist Participle, which translates, "having girded up the loins of your mind, be sober!" The word* *dianoia, suggests deep contemplation; thinking something thoroughly through in order to reach a sober conclusion! Then Peter writes, **teleios elpisate**, this is the completeness of every expectation! See Colossians 1:27. In one act of righteousness, God removed every possible definition of distance and delay! Every excuse that we could have to feel separated from God was cancelled! This is what the Prophets saw: "Every valley shall be lifted up, and every mountain and hill be made low; the crooked places shall be made straight, even the rough places shall be made smooth. And the glory of the LORD shall be revealed, and all flesh shall see it together, for the mouth of the LORD has spoken." Isaiah 40:4,5.])*

7:29 The ordinary masses of people as well as the "frowned upon" tax collectors are the ones who really heard and heeded the voice crying in the wilderness; and having been baptized by John, they showed their alliance with God's righteousness.

7:30 Meanwhile the Pharisees and the Legalists excluded themselves to their own detriment and scorned the counsel of God by rejecting John's baptism.

7:31 What is it about these people? How does one explain their indifference?

7:32 They remind me of children playing wedding and funeral games in the market squares! "Hey", they would shout to one another, "we played the flute and you wouldn't join us in the dance! We cried lamentations but you did not show any grief!" *(Instead of realizing the genius of God in this most dramatic display, they're playing their religious games. See my note on "itchy ears", 2 Tim 4:3, **knetho** from **knao**, means to tickle the ear; it suggests to be entertained rather than educated! Seneca, a famos Greek philosopher in Paul's days, uses this word and says: "Some come to hear, not to learn, just as we go to the theater, for pleasure, to delight our ears with the speaking or the voice or the plays.")*

7:33 First you have the Baptist on the stage of your entertainment and he doesn't eat bread or drink any wine - he's into fasting and no parties - and you conclude that he is crazy and most probably tormented by a demon.

7:34 Then, the son of man is the next actor on your stage, he eats and drinks and you say he is a glutton and drunkard! I mean, look at his friends, they are the scum of society - prostitutes and publicans!

7:35 Wisdom is vindicated by the fruit she bears in all her children.

Luke often highlights Jesus' social life. Jesus didn't only party with sinners and tax collectors - he often obliged the Pharisees, but never compromised his message. He now records one of three occasions where Jesus was also invited by a Pharisee for dinner. Also Luke 11:37; Luke 14:1.

7:36 One of the Pharisees [1]insisted that Jesus should come to his house for a meal. Jesus accepted the invitation and joined his table. *(The word, ηρωτα [1]erota, is in the Imperfect Tense - he insisted; repeatedly requested.)*

7:37 A woman, with a notorious reputation in the city, heard that Jesus was in town and in the Pharisees house. She arrived, [1]purposefully prepared with an alabaster flask of [2]very expensive perfume. *(The word, κολυμβάω, kolumbaō, means to care for; take care of; provide for; to take up or carry away in order to care for and preserve. [2]Alabaster, one of the precious stones used in the decoration of Solomon's Temple - 1 Chronicles 29:2. It was custom of strangers passing in and out of a house during a meal to see and converse with the guests. Trench cites a description of a dinner at a consul's house in Damietta. "Many came in and took their places on the side-seats, uninvited and yet unchallenged. They spoke to those at table on business or the news of the day, and our host spoke freely to them" ["Parables"]. Bernard beautifully says: "Thanks to thee, most blessed sinner: thou hast shown the world a safe enough place for sinners - the feet of Jesus, which spurn none, reject none, repel none, and receive and admit all.)*

7:38 Standing behind Jesus, she was weeping and her tears were like soft rain on his feet where he reclined at the table. Letting her hair down, she began to wipe away the tears with it and continued to tenderly kiss his feet and anoint them with the fragrant perfume. *(The verb, κατεφιλειis again in the Imperfect tense - to continue to - from καταφιλέω kataphileō, to kiss much, kiss again and again, kiss tenderly; ηλειφεν eleiphen, which is again the Imperfect Active [to continue to] of ἀλείφω aleiphō from a, as a particle of union and λιπαρός liparos to anoint with perfumed oil.)*

7:39 Observing all this, his host, the Pharisee, muttered to himself, "If he was the prophet he claims to be, then surely by now he would have known who and what kind of woman

this sinner is, touching and clinging to him like this!"

7:40 In answer to his thoughts Jesus said, "Simon, may I say something to you?" He replied, "Indeed Rabbi, go ahead!" *(Jesus shows that not only does he know the guy's thoughts, he is fully aware who the lady was!)*

7:41 Two people were trapped in debt to a money-lender; one owed him five hundred denarii and the other fifty. *(Denarius - containing ten units. [At one time, equal to ten asses.] It was the principal silver coin of the Roman empire. A day's wage to a laborer.)*

7:42 Neither of them could pay him back; so he frankly forgave them both. So, what would you say, which of them will love him most?"

7:43 Simon replied, "I suppose it would be the one who owed the most." "Exactly!" Jesus said.

7:44 He then turned to the woman and said to Simon, "While you are both equally debt free and neither of you are under any obligation, [1]look at her, consider how much affection and love she bestows on me! When I arrived at your house, no water was given me for my feet; but this lady washed my feet with her tears and dried them with her hair. *(Look at her! [1]blepeis. For the first time Jesus looks at the woman and he asks the Pharisee to look at her. She was behind Jesus. Jesus was an invited guest. The Pharisee had neglected some points of customary hospitality. The contrasts here made, have the rhythm of Hebrew poetry. In each contrast the first word is the point of defect in Simon: water [Luk 7:44], kiss [Luk 7:45], oil [Luk 7:46]. Robertson.)*

7:45 You didn't greet me with a kiss, but since I arrived, she hasn't stopped kissing my feet with affection!

7:46 You did not even anoint my head with oil, but she anointed my feet with fragrant ointment!

7:47 Do you now see what [1]grace means? However much [2]out of sync with her blueprint she was and however many her distortions were, she [3]had been perfectly freed of all! To be forgiven means that whatever your sins were, they no longer define you! They were and never can be who you really are! She arrived here earlier, purposefully prepared with an alabaster flask of very expensive perfume, to show how ex-travagantly much she loved me! He who does not understand the full extent of forgiveness, is like the man who shows only polite appreciation. *(The word, χαριν [1]charin, means favor; grace. The word often translated, sin, [2]hamartia, from ha, without and meros, which is the stem of the word morphe, form; thus a distorted form; the lie that we believed about ourselves. As in 2 Corinthians 3:18 the word metamorphe, with form, which is the opposite of hamartia - without form. Sin is to live out of context with the blueprint of one's design; to behave out of tune with God's original harmony. The verb, to forgive, αφεωνται [3]apheontai, is in the Perfect Passive Tense which denotes an action which is completed in the past, but the effects of which are regarded as continuing into the present without end. Nothing that happens in time could possibly intercept this! Like most Greek words, this too, is a compound word: apo, away from; and eimi, who I am. Thus, forgiveness is in essence a restoring of one's true 'I-am-ness.' The injury, insult, shame, hostility or guilt would no longer define the individual.)*

7:48 He then assured her, "You are [1]completely forgiven!" *(He again repeats this verb in the Perfect Passive - αφεωνται [2]apheontai, forgiveness is a non- negotiable, perfectly done deal!)*

7:49 This had everyone reclining at the table muttering again! "Who does this guy think he is! How dare he forgive someone like that!"

7:50 Jesus said to the woman, "Your [1]conviction of the truth, has [2]perfectly realized your salvation! [2]Bon Voyage! Journey on in this place of [3]seamless union! *(Your faith saved you! The word, [1]pistis, courageous persuasion; conviction of the truth. The verb, σεσωκεν sesoken, is the Perfect Indicative of σώζω sozo, to rescue, restore, save. The Perfect Tense realizes the completeness of the act. The verb, πορευου poreuo is a Present Imperative in the Middle Voice from [2]poreuomai, go live your life now! The middle voice giving a personal touch to it, he looked her in the eye and send her on her way. The word [3]eirene, means peace, from eiro, to join, to be set at one again; in carpentry it is the strongest joint, referred to as the dove-tail joint. Peace is a place of unhindered enjoyment of friendship beyond guilt, suspicion, blame or inferiority.)*

8:1 And thus, together with the twelve, he [1]continued his itinerary; visiting every city and village, proclaiming the wonderful news of God's Kingdom. *(The Kingdom of God within human life, is like a treasure hidden in the agricultural field; [Mt 13:44] about to be fully redeemed in human form, to be the ruling influence again in life and society. The word, καθεξῆς [1]kathexes, a word only used by Luke, 5 times in Acts and this one here; it means one after the other - according to plan; from kata, as in going beyond boundaries; throughout [every nook and cranny]; uttermost; and hexes, also a word, used only by Luke - 3 times in Acts and twice in this Gospel; from echo in the sense of taking a hold of, successively.)*

8:2 Also travelling everywhere with him were several women who were healed from evil spirits and infirmities; Mary from Magdala who was freed from tormenting demons. *(The word "seven" is used to signify that she was grievously tormented. She, Mary Magdalene, was also the first to see the risen Christ. John 20:11-18.)*

8:3 Also Joanna the wife of Chuza, Herod's steward, and Susanna, and many other women, who all participated in supporting Jesus' ministry with their gifts and belongings. *(Chusa could be the government official mentioned in John 4:46-53. It was not permitted in the culture of the time of Jesus' ministry for a woman to be mentored by a rabbi. Jesus elevated women into a place of honor and respect, in spite of the cultural limitations. These women were also the ones who provided for Jesus' care. Luke is the one Gospel writer who emphasizes Jesus' interaction with women. They would later be present at the crucifixion [Matt. 27:56; Mark 15:40-41; Luke 23:49, 5] and his glorious resurrection. [Luke 24:1-11])*

8:4 Large crowds from many of the surrounding villages and cities kept [1]flocking together in their [2]pursuit of him; he [3]told them the following illustration: *(The word, συνιοντος from [1]suneimi, with the components, sun, together and eimi, "I am" denoting the idea of, "common ground". Then, επιπορευομενων from, [2]epiporeuomai; both words, again, only used by Luke, are Present Participles, meaning, something in progress; they kept flocking and clustering together in their common attraction to Jesus.)*

8:5 Picture a sower who goes out to sow his seed and some landed on a pathway where it was trodden under foot and eaten by birds.

8:6 Some seed landed on rocky soil where it begins to grow briefly, then for lack of moisture, it would wither up and die.

8:7 Still, other seed fell amongst thorny weeds where it became strangled.

8:8 But the seed which lands in good soil, flourishes and yields a return of a hundred to one! He then cried out with a loud voice, "Now listen up with your inner ears! It is how you hear my word that makes all the difference!" *(Note, seed in singular throughout the parable - reminding of Galatians 3:16, It is on record that the promise [of the blessing of righteousness by God's faith] was made to Abraham and to his seed, singular, [thus excluding his effort to produce Ishmael.] Isaac, the child of promise and not of the flesh, mirrors the Messiah.)*

8:9 The disciples wanted to know what he meant by this parable.

8:10 He told them, you were already given insight to understand the mystery of the kingdom of God *[in your close association with me]* but I speak in parables to those, who see and hear yet struggle to comprehend.

8:11 This is what the parable means, God's conversation with mankind is the seed.

8:12 The seed on the road means that some hear the word, then because of a typical [1]inferior mindset, it is stolen from their hearts before it germinates and they remain trapped in their unbelief. *(The word, [1]diabolos, from dia, because of, and ballo, cast down. Thus, a mindset ruled by the "I am-not-Tree." See James 1:24.)*

8:13 The rocky soil represent the ones who hear and receive the word with joy; but because they have no root to anchor them, their belief is brief and in times of temptation they fall away.

8:14 Then there is the seed that landed up amongst thorny bushes; they are the ones who also hear the word, but, in the course of life, the typical [1]distractions that are associated with the pursuit of wealth and pleasures, suffocate them before any fruit matures. *(The word, [1]merimna, from merizo, to divide, distract.)*

8:15 But the seed in the good soil are those who hear [1]in such a way, that the word finds a consistent and beautiful [1]resonance in their hearts. They are the ones who continue to bear fruit in steadfast resolve. *(The word ¹katechō, to hold fast; to check a ship's headway, i.e. to hold or head the ship.)*

8:16 No one lights a lamp only to cover it again under a kitchen utensil, or hide it under a bed! It is placed on a stand to give maximum light to all who enter the house. *(The incarnation is not to hide, but to unveil the mystery that was hidden for ages and generations! See verse 18!)*

8:17 There is nothing hidden that will not become fully known; even things that have long been unnoticed will come to light! *(The full counsel of God is destined to flood the earth with the knowledge of his glory unveiled in human life! And all flesh shall see it together! Isa 40:5)*

8:18 It is therefore most important that you hear in such a way that what you have already grasped, becomes fully unveiled in you; don't think that, just because you have heard something that sounded convincing at the time, it will go unchallenged! You may even assume that you've grasped it, but then, when contradictions come, you're not so sure anymore! *(The lamp is lit, but then domestic issues in the house my hide it from view! See verse 16.)*

8:19 His mother and siblings arrived but could not reach him because of the multitude. *(Luke immediately takes us to Jesus' own domestic issues! See Luke 9:58, "Foxes have holes, and birds of the air have nests, but the Son of Man has nowhere to lay his head.")*

8:20 He was told that they were standing outside and wished to see him.

8:21 To which he responded, my mother and immediate family are those who keep hearing and consistently and fully engage my word without hesitance. *(The words akouontes ἀκούοντες and poiountes ποιοῦντες are both in the Present Active Participle form of the verb to emphasize a continual or habitual hearing and engaging.)*

8:22 On a certain day, he suggested to his disciples that they cross the lake by boat. *(See Luke 5:1 Lake Gennesaret. It seems that Jesus deliberately chose a day where the predictions [according to seasoned fishermen] did not look promising!)*

8:23 While sailing, he fell into a deep sleep. Suddenly a massive storm broke upon them and the raging waves were surging dangerously over the boat and filling it with water.

8:24 They awoke him with urgent cries, "[1]Captain, Captain, we are drowning!" And he [2]rose up to face the storm and ordered the wind and waves to be quiet, and immediately there was a great calm. *(Only Luke uses this name for Jesus, [7 times in his gospel]* [1]*epistata εnιστατα, εnιστατα - the one who stands in front; teacher; master; captain of the ship - See chapter 5:5, Simon announces Jesus the Skipper of his boat! Luke then uses the word* [2]*diegeiro, to arise - often used of an agitated sea rising in a storm [see John 6:18] - Jesus arose in authority - not in a shock response to the violent weather! Same word Peter uses in 2 Pet 1:13...I desire to stir you up by way of reminder!)*

8:25 Jesus then addressed them, "So the size of the storm totally dwarfed your faith into insignificance?" *(The word,* **pou** *is the genitive case of an interrogative pronoun of amount,* **posos**, *great, much.)*

8:26 They then arrived on the shores of Gerasa which lies directly across the Lake from Galilee. *(Dr. Thomson discovered by the lake, the ruins of Khersa [Gerasa]. This village is in the district of the city of Gadara some miles southeastward.)*

8:27 And a local man approached Jesus; he was harassed by demons for many years. He lived amongst the tombs, naked and homeless.

8:28 When he saw Jesus he cried out and fell prostrate before him. He cried out with a loud voice, "Why are you doing this to me, Jesus, son of the Most High God? I pray that you do not [1]torment me!" *(The word* [1]*basanizō, is an old verb, to test metals; from* **basis** *- to get to the bottom of a thing; often associated with the idea of torment. See my notes on Rev 14:10 re the touchstone. Rev 4:9 Then a third celestial shepherd-messenger followed and announced with a loud voice that whoever worships the counterfeit lamb and its image and receives its character in their thoughts and deeds, Rev 14:10 will drink the wine of God's passion, undiluted with water but intensified with spices in his cup - they shall be tested as one tests gold or silver with a touchstone; with fire and brimstone in the immediate presence of the Lamb and of those who have discovered their wholeness mirrored in him - the dross of their deception will be exposed and cleansed!*

116

The unclean spirits knew that their time of abusing people was over! Here they were confronted and judged by the Incarnate Word, destined to be the slain and risen Lamb of God.)

8:29 Jesus already told the unclean spirit to depart from the man. For it would often seize him; then people would tie him down with chains and fetters while guarding over him. But he would frequently break out and the demon would forcefully drive him into remote places.

8:30 Jesus then asked him what his name was and he answered, "Legion", because many demons entered him. *(The single unclean spirit, typical of a virus, multiplies only in a host body - Scientists estimate that there are roughly 10^{31} viruses at any given moment! That is a one, with 31 zeroes after it! If it was possible to line up these viruses, the virus column would extend nearly 200 light years into space. There are over ten million times more viruses on earth than there are stars in the entire universe. Because they can't reproduce by themselves [without a host], viruses are not considered living. Viruses reproduce by infecting their host cells and reprogramming them to become virus-making "factories." Thoughts that spring from the "I-am-not-Tree system", multiplies into thought patterns which become strongholds! Paul declares, that we are empowered in Christ, to disengage mindsets [strongholds], by taking individual thoughts captive; these include any thought that set itself up against what God knows to be true about us, as evidenced in Christ! See 2 Cor 10:3, The fact that we are living in a physical world in human bodies of flesh does not mean that we engage ourselves in a combat dictated to by the typical "tit-for-tat" strategies of religion and the politics of the day. 2 Cor 10:4 The dynamic of our strategy is revealed in God's ability to disengage mindsets and perceptions that have held people captive in pseudo fortresses for centuries! 2 Cor 10:5 Every lofty idea and argument positioned against God's knowledge of us, is cast down and exposed to be a mere invention of our own imagination. We [1]arrest every thought at spear point - anything that could possibly trigger an opposing threat to our redeemed identity and innocence! The caliber of our weapon is empowered by the revelation of the ultimate consequence of the obedience of Christ. [The obedience of Christ dwarfs the effect of the disobedience of Adam into insignificance! See Romans 5:12-21. The word **aichmalōtizō** from **aichme**, spear and **halosis**, to capture, thus, to arrest at spear point.]*

These vast numbers sound similar to Rev 9:16 And I heard the number of the armies of the cavalry which amounted to two myriads of myriads which is two hundred million horsemen! [This is an immense and unparalleled number of horsemen. Ten thousand times ten thousand is one hundred million; consequently the number here referred to would be 200 million. The Japanese also has a highest value of ten thousand and their next highest would be ten thousand times ten thousand which is a hundred million. Countless - 2 myriads - literally ten thousands times ten thousands and thousands of thousands! The largest number named in Ancient Greek was the myriad-myriad [written MM] or hundred million. In his Sand Reckoner, Archimedes of Syracuse used this quantity as the basis for a numeration system of large powers of ten, which he used to count grains of sand! According to PIE, the etymology of the word myriad has been variously connected to meu- "damp" in reference to the waves of the sea and to Greek myrmex [μύρμηξ, "ant"] in reference to their swarms. Proto-Indo-European [PIE] is the linguistic reconstruction of the common ancestor of the Indo-European languages, the most widely spoken language family in the world.])

8:31 And they begged Jesus not to order them to descend into the Abyss. *(In Mark's rendering of this incident, they ask Jesus to, not send them out of the "country" - Mark 5:10, the word, χώρα - chōra, translated, country, means a space lying between two places or limits. Now, the unclean spirits were already confined to the earth-dimension [See Rev 12:7-9]; the earth realm was surrounded by the heavenly realm and the great abyss, the under-world. Their only alternative was either the ocean or the abyss!*

In Rom 10:7, Paul uses the word, Hades, to which Christ descended. See Revelation chapter 9 as well as the commentary notes on the Abyss in the Mirror Bible. See Phil 2:10,11.

Also, my commentary on Armageddon in Rev 16. In the symbolic language of the book of Revelation people's perception of the world is four dimensional: heaven, earth, the ocean and the deep underworld [including under the ocean.] Eze 28:8; Rev 5:13. The idea of the earth dwellers of the time was that the planet was flat and square! So the four corners of the earth were not factual but merely to communicate a symbolic picture and principle within their perceptions - as also the idea of an under world. See these spheres already referenced in Gen 1:2, the earth being without form and empty, and darkness on the face of the deep, [abussos - LXX] and the Spirit of God moving gently on the face of the waters. Also in Ps 135:6 Whatever the LORD pleases he does, in heaven and on earth, in the seas and the abyss. Or in the LXX it is Ps 134:6.

118

Armageddon pictures the battle between the lower, earthbound thought patterns and the elevated, heavenly thoughts of God. Col 3:1-3; Rev 17:8.

The "earthbound-dilemma" of mankind is fully addressed in the Incarnate Christ. The language of the Book of Revelation is purely symbolic. Its rich imagery celebrates the Champion of the Ages, the slain and risen Lamb of God bringing closure to every idea of judgment, in his death and resurrection.

Jesus is not a literal Lamb, nor a literal Lion! As the Son of God he is the Incarnate Word that has always been face to face with God. He is the Word in whom all things exist!

The stars are not literal stars neither is the underworld a literal fathomless pit, or the Lake ablaze with Brimstone a literal "geographic" place!

Throughout the unfolding conversation, pictures come to mind that have already been part of the narrative of God's prophetic dealings with Israel for generations, symbolically pointing to a Person and a moment recorded historically in time, where the resolve of God concludes powerfully in the glorious triumph of the Lamb over every definition of Devil. [See 1 Pet 1:10,11] In fact, every possible idea of Sin, Judgment, Death, Hades, Satan, Devil, Demon, Dragon, Beast and False Prophet - Prostitute is addressed and dissolved and thus rendered redundant. See Rev 17:14 These join forces in that hour to wage war against the Lamb, but the Lamb defeats them since he is the Lord of lords and the King of kings. And, sharing with him in his victory, are his kindred, recognizing their origin in this conversation; they too are now of the same persuasion. The Lamb led them into freedom from their lost identity, and their doubts.)

8:32 Then, Jesus, upon their request, sent them into the large herd of pigs grazing on the mountain.

8:33 Thus the demons were expelled from the man and entered into the swine; and the herd was hurled impetuously over the precipice into the Lake and drowned.

8:34 Those tending the pigs ran for their lives and spread the news everywhere in the towns and farms.

8:35 Many people responded and went out to see what had happened; they were awestruck when they saw the man freed from demons, clothed and his mind fully restored; he was sitting at the feet of Jesus.

8:36 Those who witnessed the event, told everyone how this demon possessed man was rescued.

8:37 Then the entire population of the Gerasenes, including the adjacent districts, begged Jesus to depart from them; for they were gripped with great fear. So he boarded the ship to return to Galilee. *(Again, sadly, the typical response of a sin-conscious ruled community - they obviously felt more comfortable with things as it was before Jesus arrived! Plus, healing the demoniac was not good for business! The Gerasenes, was located in the territory of the Decapolis, a group of ten cities with a majority population of Gentiles. No Jewish farmer would keep swine, and no Jewish region would tolerate the presence of pigs, let alone two thousand of them!)*

8:38 All along, the man who was delivered, begged him to take him with him; but Jesus sent him back with this instruction,

8:39 "Return to your home and [1]give a bold account to everyone of what God has done [2]in you!" So he went and proclaimed throughout the entire city everything that Jesus had done [2]in him. *(The word, διηγου [1]diegou, from διά, dia through, and ήγέομαι, hegeomai, to lead with distinction; with the idea of thoroughness. A strengthened form of the word agoo, to lead; thus, to be officially appointed in a position of authority. To lead or carry a narration through to the end. Dr. Luke was familiar with this terminology. The word, diegou was particularly applied to a medical treatise. Galen applies it at least seventy-three times to the writings of Hippocrates. [Vincent]*

The words, σοι [2]soi, and again, αυτω [2]autoo, are Personal Pronouns in the Dative case, indirect object, "to"; also location "in".

Some interesting observations about Hippocrates: He was the Father of Western Medicine - he died at 90, 460 - 370 BC. Born on the island of Kos, Greece. He based his medical practice on observations and on the study of the human body. He held the belief that illness had a physical and a rational explanation. He rejected the views of his time that considered illness to be caused by superstitions and by possession of evil spirits and disfavor of the gods. Disease was not a punishment inflicted by the gods but rather the product of environmental factors, diet, and living habits. He believed in the natural healing process of rest, a good diet, fresh air and cleanliness. In general, the Hippocratic medicine was very kind to the patient; treatment was gentle, and emphasized keeping the patient clean and sterile. For example, only clean water or wine were ever used on wounds, though "dry" treatment was preferable. Soothing balms were sometimes employed. Hippocrates was reluctant to administer drugs and engage in specialized treatment that might prove to be wrongly chosen. Generalized treatments he prescribed included fasting and the consumption of a mix of honey and vinegar. Hippocrates once said that "to eat when you are sick, is to feed your sickness." He noted that there were individual differences in the severity of disease symptoms and that some individuals were better able to cope with their disease and illness than others. He was also the first physician that held the belief that thoughts, ideas, and feelings come from the brain and not the heart as others of his time believed.

The ministry of Jesus, as also emphasized by Dr Luke, far exceeds medication or medical diagnosis and explanations. See verse 43.)

8:40 The crowds welcomed Jesus warmly on his return to Galilee, since they were all ¹looking out for him with eager expectancy. *(Here Luke uses the Periphrastic Imperfect Active of ¹prosdokaō, an old verb for eager expectancy.)*

8:41 Then, a man by the name of Jairus, the chief of the synagogue, approached him with a most urgent request; he collapsed at the feet of Jesus begging him to come to promptly come to his house.

8:42 His only daughter, and only twelve years old, was dying. Jesus immediately went with him but the dense crowd was thronging them.

8:43 Amongst them was a woman who was suffering from an issue of blood for twelve years; she had spent all she owned on physicians, but not one of them could heal her. *(Interesting in the context of my comments on Hippocrates in verse 39, her physicians obviously also studied and were certainly influenced by Hippocrates; as was Dr. Luke for that matter. However, Luke records the healing ministry of Jesus which far eclipses the dimension of medical as well as natural cures.)*

8:44 She squeezed though the throng of people and touched the hem of Jesus' garment and was instantly cured!

8:45 Surprisingly, Jesus immediately wanted to know who it was that touched him. But no one stepped forward; then Peter said to him, how can you ask that? Throngs of people are crowding you and many are obviously touching you! *(The word, ἅπτομαι ¹haptomai, means to touch, to clasp, to cling to; it is the reflexive form of ἅπτω haptō, to kindle, light a fire.)*

8:46 Jesus answered, "Someone has touched me differently; I felt a surge of power emanating from me."

8:47 Then, realizing that she could not remain unnoticed, she approached Jesus, trembling and knelt before him and proceeded to tell everyone her story and that she felt heat going though her body as she touched the hem of his garment and was [1]instantly [2]cured! *(The word, παραχρῆμα [1]parachrēma, immediately, is used only 19 times in the NT - twice by Matthew but 17 times by Luke. Again Luke uses the word, ἰάομαι [2]iaomai to heal, from ἰαίνω iaínō, "to warm". Of the 29 times this word is used in the NT, Luke uses it 17 times - as medical man he is interested to know how someone feels who experiences the healing touch of Jesus! This is amazing! Also in my own experience, when praying with people, I have had people testify that they felt heat moving through their bodies or in the affected areas! I believe, that even while reading the Mirror Bible, unveiled understanding comes to you and faith and healing happens! I do not imply that someone has to "feel" the heat in order to be healed! Many times healing happens without any "feeling"!*

See also Luke 6:18,19 Everyone in the crowd was pressing in to touch him, because power was surging from him and he healed them all, one by one. [The word, ἅπτομαι haptomai, means to cling to; attach oneself to; from ἅπτω haptō, to kindle a fire! Then the sentence, δύναμις παρ' αὐτοῦ ἐξήρχετο - dunamis para auto eksercheto, - para, closest possible proximity of nearness - out of his innermost being. Then, kai iāto pantas - with ιατο in the Imperfect Middle voice, he kept on healing every single one; the Middle voice giving a personal touch to it all.])

8:48 And he said to her, Daughter, your persuasion saved you, continue on your life's journey [1]in this place of our [2]joint-oneness and peace. *(The preposition [1]eis, speaks of a point reached in conclusion. The word, [2]eirene, means peace, from eiro, to join, to be set at one again, in carpentry it is referred to as the dove-tail joint, which is the strongest joint. Peace is a place of unhindered enjoyment of friendship beyond guilt, suspicion, blame or inferiority.)*

8:49 Jesus was [1]still speaking *[to the woman he healed from a 12 year long condition]* when someone arrived to tell the ruler of the synagogue that his daughter had died and that there would be no further need to trouble the Teacher. *(Luke uses the Present Active Participle, [1]lalountos, λαλουντος, of the verb, λαλέω. I just love Luke's attention to detail! He positions Jairus in the middle of this conversation! See next verse also...)*

8:50 Jesus, overhearing the conversation said to the Ruler, "You have no need to be disturbed by this news! [1]Remain in this place of seamless persuasion and she shall be completely restored." *(Hah! Luke again emphasizes Jairus' inclusion in the immediate audience! Jesus overheard..." Jairus has just heard the testimony of the lady who was instantly healed from a condition that she suffered from for 12 years! As long as his daughter was old! This must have so impacted his faith! The word, [1]monon, from μένω meno, to abide; to continue to be present; abiding in seamless union.*

I love Dr. Luke! He again and again reminds us in Jesus' conversation, that it is vitally important "how" you hear! Mere, academic hearing just doesn't do it! Debating and arguing neither. And in this case, don't let bad news interrupt your hearing!)

8:51 When they got to the house he would not let anyone in except Peter, James and John, as well as the father and mother of the girl.

8:52 Everyone outside was weeping and overcome with grief, but Jesus said, there is no need for weeping since she is only sleeping and not dead!

8:53 Their wailing immediately became scornful laughter since they were convinced that she was dead.

8:54 He then grabbed her hand firmly and summoned her, "Little lady, arise!"

8:55 Her spirit immediately returned and she stood up! Jesus then suggested that they bring her something to eat.

8:56 Her parents were besides themselves with joy! He then insisted that it was not necessary to elaborate on any detail of what had happened in the room.

 Lydia and Francois met on the 25th of August 1974, while he was working with Youth For Christ. She was sixteen and he nineteen! The following year he studied Greek and Hebrew at the University of Pretoria for three years while Lydia completed her nursing training. In 1978 Francois also spent a year with Youth with a Mission. They married in January 1979 and are blessed with four amazing children, Renaldo, Tehilla, Christo and Stefan; also, two darling grandchildren Nicola and Christiaan.

They worked in a full-time mission for fourteen years, during which time they also pastored a church and led a training facility for more than 700 students over a five-year period. They then left the ministry and for ten years did business mainly in the tourism industry. They built and managed a Safari Lodge in the Sabi Sand Game Reserve and eventually relocated to Hermanus where they started Southern Right Charters boat-based whale watching.

In December 2000 Francois began to write the book, "God believes in You" which led to him being invited to speak at various Christian camps and churches. Since February 2004, they travelled regularly abroad and into Africa as well as South Africa.

Francois has written several books in both English and Afrikaans, including God Believes in You, Divine Embrace, The Logic of His Love and The Eagle Story; these are also available on Kindle. Also Kant En Klaar [Done!]

In order to focus their time on writing and translation, they relocated from Hermanus in 2015 to a remote farm in the Swartberg Mountains. They have also stopped most of their travelling.

Lydia has written 6 amazing children's stories of which Stella's Secret, The Little Bear And The Mirror, Kaa of the Great Kalahari as well as The Eagle Story, are already published in print and on Kindle. Her most recent story "King Solitaire's Banquet" will be released soon.

Francois continues to be passionately engaged in his translation of the Mirror Bible, which will eventually include the entire NT as well as select portions of the old. The 1st 250 page A5 Edition was published in 2012.

Lydia's books are already available in English Afrikaans, German and Spanish.

The Mirror Bible is currently available in Spanish, Shona, Xhosa and large portions in German.

Thousands of people subscribe to their daily posts on Social Media; Lydia has her own fb page and Francois has 5 English pages on Facebook.

You can get more detail about them on **www.mirrorword.net**

The Mirror Bible is also on Kindle as well as an App, **app.mirrorword.net**

REFERENCES and RESOURCES

Referred to by the author's name or by some abridgment of the title.

Adam Clarke (1762–1832 A British Methodist theologian)

Ackerman *[Christian Element in Plato]*

Bruce Metzger *(Textual Commentary on the Greek NT)*

Barnes Notes (Notes on the Bible, by Albert Barnes, [1834], at sacred-texts. com)

BBE (1949, Bible in Basic English)

Doddrich (Philip Doddridge 1702-1751 www.ccel.org/d/doddridge)

Dr. Robinson (Greek Lexicon by Edward Robinson1851)

E-Sword by Rick Meyers (www.e-sword.net)

J.H. Thayer (Greek-English Lexicon of the New Teatament By Joseph Henry Thayer, DD - Edinburgh - T&T CLARK - Fourth Edition 1901)

J.B. Phillips Translation (Geoffrey Bles London 1960)

Jeff Benner http://www.ancient-hebrew.org/

KJV (King James Version - In 1604, King James I of England authorized that a new translation of the Bible into English. It was finished in 1611)

Knox Translation (Translated from the Vulgate Latin by Ronald Knox Published in London by Burns Oates and Washbourne Ltd. 1945)

Marvin R. Vincent (1834-1922) Word Studies.

NEB (New English Bible New Testament - Oxford & Cambridge University Press 1961)

Robert Charles *R. H. (Robert Henry), 1855-1931*

RSV (The Revised Standard Version is an authorized revision of the American Standard Version, published in 1901, which was a revision of the King James Version, published in 1611.)

Strongs (James Strong - Dictionary of the Bible)

The Message (Eugene H. Peterson Nav Press Publishing Group)

Walter Bauer (Greek English Lexicon - a translation of Walter Bauer's Griechisch-Deutches Worterbuch by Arndt and Gingrich 1958)

Wesley J. Perschbacher (The New Analytical Greek Lexicon Copyright 1990 by Hendrickson Publishers, Inc)

Westcott and Hort *The New Testament in the Original Greek 1881*

Weymouth New Testament *(M.A., D.Lit. 1822-1902)*

Zodhiates Complete Word Study Lexicon Mantis Bible Study for Apple